STILL a STUPID MAN

Semi-Retired/Semi-Employed
& Loving Life

By
Mike Turnbull

You are in God's Country! Enjoy!

Mike Turnbull
10-8-21

PREFACE

I am not exactly sure why yet, but I am going to continue writing down "Random Thoughts." This will be my third book; I will decide on a title when it comes to me. The first book was titled *Random Thoughts of a Stupid Man*; the second book was brilliantly titled *More Random Thoughts of a Stupid Man*. Both books were published by Rivershore Books and are available through them, Amazon, and Barnes & Noble. If you haven't read them, please consider doing so.

I am hoping that this book will be published by Rivershore Books also, otherwise I am just sitting here at my computer typing yet more "Random Thoughts of a Stupid Man" for no apparent reason other than my own enjoyment. If that is the case, I'm still going to keep going because I do enjoy writing. I can only hope you find some joy in reading what I write.

DEDICATION

I want to dedicate *Still a Stupid Man* to Beckett Michael Baack, born on June 23, 2015.

Beckett is my first grandchild, and I couldn't be prouder. I love you and I love being "Grandpa Mike"! I can't wait until you can say "Grandpa Mike."

I also want to warn you that you are destined to also be a "Stupid Man." I'm sure your Great-Great-Grandpa Herb was accused of being stupid. I know your Great-Grandpa Jack, my father, was tagged with the title. I can guarantee you that your Grandpa Mike has been called stupid on many occasions. I'm not sure where your Great-Grandpa Rod stands. You'll have to ask your Great-Grandma Tootsie. I think your dad is a strong candidate for the "Stupid Man" club. Your mom will let you know. Your Uncle Blaine and your great uncles will all be members in due time. You can check with your Grandpa Jim.

Take pride in it. We will all welcome you with open arms when it is confirmed by the women in your life that you deserve to be enshrined in the "Stupid Man" club.

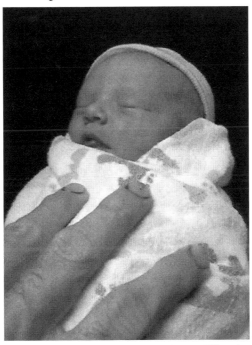

Beckett Michael Baack, born June 23, 2015. That is my hand.
(Photo by Pam Turnbull)

4/17/2014

My wife and I left Hibbing, MN, at 12:30 today to pick up our son Blaine in Minneapolis. We are all driving to Auburn, NE, to see our daughter (Blaine's sister) and her husband Jeff for the Easter weekend. My wife says this will be fun because we haven't all been together for Easter since Lexie and Jeff got married five years ago. Also, neither one of us can remember the last time we did any traveling with Blaine. I just hope Blaine can handle a road trip with his parents!

4/18/2014

We stayed at the Hotel Pattee in Perry, IA, last night—Pam's choice. Blaine and I were a little skeptical, but we both have to admit, Pam nailed it. The HP was a great little boutique hotel and was decorated immaculately. I can't believe I just said that out loud!

We are driving to Kansas City today; I was relieved to hear they arrested the guy who was shooting at people on the highways in the Kansas City area, since that should make for a much safer visit.

4/19/2014

Great day yesterday; Pam was happy—she got to tour a mansion and Harry Truman's home in Independence, MO. Blaine, Pam, and I all enjoyed touring the Harry Truman Presidential Library, and dinner at the Café Verona afterward was outstanding. Blaine and I capped off the day by attending a Royals and Twins baseball game at Kaufman Stadium. I had never seen a game there before—nice park. We tailgated a little before the game. That was fun except for running into all the Twins haters. I don't always like the way the Twins play, either, but Royals fans flat-out hate on the Twins. I think it is because for several years the Twins beat the Royals on a regular basis, but that is not the case now and it definitely wasn't last night; Royals 5 and Twins 0.

4/20/2014

Today was definitely out of the ordinary. Blaine, my son-in-law Jeff, and I went to Lincoln, NE, and watched the University of Nebraska play Northwestern University in baseball today. Afterwards we met up with Pam and Lexie, who had been shopping, and went out for dinner.

The weather was great, the game was a good one, and dinner was fabulous, but the highlight of the day was the men's urinal at Longwell's in Haymarket Square in downtown Lincoln. I know there was a tongue-in-cheek commercial on television a couple years ago that said, "What happens in Lincoln, stays in Lincoln," but I have to share this one. Keep in mind, I don't get out much and I am easily amused. Anyway, after a couple of excellent micro-brews at Longwell's, I needed to go to the bathroom. I am 55 now, so that happens sooner than it used to. There was a video screen located about chest high just above the urinal, displaying advertisements. I had seen that before, but this was special. When you started to pee, a video game kicked in and all of a sudden you were virtually riding a motorcycle and shooting (peeing on) penguins. You received one point each time you hit one and your score was tabulated. I have always liked penguins, but I quickly put that sentiment out of my head and went for the kill shots. Who would have ever guessed you could have so much fun in Lincoln, NE. For the record, I made three more trips to the bathroom and my high score was 27! It left me to wonder, how much easier would potty training boys be if this game could be incorporated into potty chairs?

4/22/2014

Easter Sunday came and went yesterday. We went to sunrise service and had lunch with Jeff's family out at a friend's farm. We topped the night off at Lexie and Jeff's, playing Hollywood Game Night, which Lexie and Jeff had given to me for my birthday. I don't care what anyone says; it is extremely difficult to hum a song to your teammates when all you can use is the word "Do." You try humming "My Girl" by the Temptations and remember you can only use the word "Do." It is one of my favorite songs, but I couldn't do it.

Pam, Blaine, and I drove back to Minnesota today and dropped off Blaine in Minneapolis around 3:00, and Pam and I arrived in Hibbing around 8:00. All in all, a very enjoyable trip and it was great to spend quality time with our kids. Being the "Stupid Man" that I am, though, I still have to say, the game in the urinal at Longwell's is right near the top of my list of highlights. Like I said, I don't get out much and I am easily amused.

4/26/2014

Big change in my life today. Our men's basketball coach resigned today and I will be moving from coaching the women's program to coaching the men's program. Let's just say I am now the new/old men's basketball coach at Hibbing CC.

I met with my women's team at 8:30 this morning to give them the news. Without being too emotional, I will just say that it was not easy. I do know they are in good hands, though; Kate Brau is the new women's coach and she will do a great job. Now the work starts. I was all but done recruiting the women's 2014–15 team and now I have to start over and recruit the 2014–15 men's team. It will be a challenge, but I am extremely excited about it and looking forward to the challenge.

I have always felt that change and new challenges in our life are good things. They help us grow and take away the stagnation that can enter into our lives.

5/2/2014

Pam and I are in the process of trying to buy a cabin on Fall Lake just outside of Winton, MN. I know; where is Winton, MN? It is just a couple of miles past Ely, MN, on Highway 169. If you are ever in Ely, drive down Sheridan street, continue past Skube's Bait Shop, past the Dorothy Molter Museum and Wolf Center, go about two more miles on 169, and Winton is off to your left.

We have run into a couple of hold-ups; inspections of the cabin, well, and septic, along with a couple of—hopefully minor—property line encroachments were discovered when a new survey was conducted. We are both hoping all this can be cleared up quickly and we can finalize the purchase. Up until today, I have tried to curtail my excitement and not get too far ahead of myself. I really don't want to jinx anything. I have set aside some clothes and tools I want to take to the cabin, but other than that no purchases. Pam, on the other hand, has been sorting clothes, linens, furniture, decorative items, dishware, etc. That brings me to today. I cracked—I bought a new trolling motor at L&M Supply and I am fired up about it. Technically it is not for the cabin; it is for my boat. Hopefully, this will not bring about any bad voodoo as far as the cabin purchase is concerned. I do know, though, that as soon as the purchase is finalized, I am going to look at a Boat-Lift to put by the dock that already exists.

I have dreamed of having a place by the lake ever since I moved out of my mom and dad's house on Farm Lake. So, to say the least, it is pretty cool to think that Pam and I are this close to buying a cabin.

On a completely different note, I participated in the ultimate Iron Range experience for men, especially for "Stupid Men." I went to a Men's Health seminar. My wife thought it would be a good idea for me personally and professionally (I teach wellness, physical education, and psychology). The seminar was held at the Municipal Building, just two blocks from our house, so it was very convenient to walk over and check it out. The irony in the whole experience was that pizza and beer was served before it was time to file into the Little Theater to listen to the guest speaker. I am going to venture a guess and say that there can't be too many places outside of the Iron Range in northern Minnesota where free beer and pizza are served at a Health Seminar. Bottom line, it was well attended and whatever gets men to sit down and listen to a health lecture can't be completely bad.

At one point in the lecture, the speaker, Rod Raymond, said that we live 95% of our life in the subconscious brain. I'm pretty sure this is about the time that the subconscious thought, "I have to pee," moved to my conscious brain, so I politely left the room and went to the bathroom. I am also pretty sure when I was standing at the urinal, my subconscious brain was probably wishing we were back at Longwell's peeing on penguins.

When I returned to the lecture, Dr. Raymond was explaining that in one minute's time our brain is capable of forming about twelve conscious thoughts and in that same one minute's time processes about 40,000 subconscious thoughts. The trick is to try to bring as many subconscious thoughts into the conscious realm as possible. I tried, it stressed me out, and I lost focus on what he was saying. About the time I became refocused, he threw another factoid at us: 90% of doctor's visits are a result of stress. I was just thinking; if we could just stay in the subconscious as much as possible, maybe we would experience less stress. I have been accused several times of being a dreamer. Maybe that is not a bad thing. Dreaming has never been stressful to me; trying to live those dreams and working to get them to come to fruition is where the stress enters into my life. The next time you ask someone how they are doing and they say, "I am just living the dream!" your next question should be "How are you dealing with the stress?"

5/3/2014

Pam and I have several guests staying at the Bed & Breakfast this weekend. Three of those guests are associated with the Shrine Circus that is in town this weekend. One of them is the manager of the Jose Coles' Circus; her daughter is an aerialist and her son manages the concessions. I bring this up because I asked one of them earlier today how they were doing, and their response was, "Life is a circus!" I realize many of us say this from time to time, but these people mean it, and in their case, it is an absolute truth.

5/11/2014

Today was Mother's Day — shout out to all the moms — I hope you all had a great day! I called my mom in Minneapolis this morning; she was glad to hear from her (only) son and I enjoyed visiting with her. I was unable to go see her today, but my son, Blaine, and his girlfriend had her over to their place and cooked brunch for her. This should solidify Blaine as the "Golden Grandchild." Why not? He is the son of the "Golden Child"!

Today is also our daughter's 31st birthday. When I look in the mirror I see a guy that definitely could have a 31-year-old daughter. When I look at my wife, I don't see a woman who is the mother of a 31-year-old daughter. Pam is only a year younger than myself and I know she is the mother of both of our kids. She has just aged better than me. I live a good life; where is the justice?

Pam and I went to Ely today to see her mom. We spent a little over an hour walking around the property at the prospective cabin on Fall Lake. We both love it there. I sure hope we finalize this purchase soon. It was a beautiful morning at the lake; the ice just went off a couple of days ago, so we were able to get a good look at the lakeshore. It is going to be great!

After looking around at the lake, we went back into town and met up with Pam's family and had brunch at the Grand Ely Lodge. I had the pleasure of experiencing another great non-Facebook moment. I ran into Jimmy Joe Grahek, an ex-high school baseball teammate. I hadn't seen him in a couple of years, so it was great catching up. We made plans to get together at the cabin on the 4th of July. We'd better get this thing bought.

Jim was with his wife and mom and at the table next to them was the Katauskas family, Len, Pat, and their son Steve. Len and Pat were my bosses at Kat's Liquor Store in Ely. I worked at Kat's while I was in college and the first couple of summers after I started teaching. This was sort of a strange circle to connect. I moved to Ely my junior year of high school in 1975. The first place I ever made an underage beer purchase at was Kat's Drive-In Liquor and Jimmy Joe was driving. I'm pretty sure that didn't come up during my job interview with Len and Pat, and I'm pretty sure I never shared this story with them. I didn't share this story today, but I started thinking about it on our drive back to Hibbing tonight.

Tomorrow is the start of the last week of classes at the college. Normally, I would just be in wrap-up mode and planning my summer schedule. This week will be more challenging. I had a slight change in my job description a couple of weeks ago, and I am preparing to coach the men's basketball team.

I am hoping to finish my personal interviews with the possible returning players this week and figure out who wants to return. I will also continue recruiting incoming freshmen and will be working on that all summer. I like where we are headed with the basketball program, but we really won't know what we have until the spring and summer semesters end, because several of the prospective sophomores have to pull better grades to be eligible. So, once again, my livelihood is back in the hands of 18- to 20-year-old men and how they perform in the classroom. We can worry about the basketball court after we see the grades. It really doesn't matter how talented a college athlete is; if they don't pull good grades in the classroom, you'll never see them on the court or field. This is a tough lesson for some of these kids to learn.

5/15/2014

Note the date, May 15th; It is 8:30 AM. It is snowing! Are you kidding me?

5/30/2014

One of my dreams became a reality today; Pam and I closed on the cabin on Fall Lake today. We are officially cabin owners. We will decide later if we are calling it a cabin or a lake place; for now let's just go with cabin.

Our son Blaine came up for the Memorial Day weekend and he and I will stay at the cabin for the next couple of nights. Pam had to go back to Hibbing to check some guests in at our Bed & Breakfast. Before she left, we had her mom and dad out here for supper and a small celebration. We will never be able to thank Rod, Pam's dad, enough for making the cabin purchase possible. Some Sir G's Pizza and champagne doesn't cut it, but it will be a start.

6/6/2014

I cut the grass at the cabin today. I got something in my eye, or at least had the sensation I had something in my eye.

6/7/2014

Woke up this morning with a bump above my right eye. I assumed it was a spider bite.

6/8/2014

My forehead is swelling, my right eye is closing, and I feel like my scalp is on fire. I went to Shopko in Ely and picked up eye drops and Neonephrine; hopefully it helps.

6/9/2014

Woke up this morning and my condition is worse. I broke down and went to the Ely Hospital to get it checked out. Turns out I have Shingles! I wouldn't wish this on my worst enemy. This is the worst pain I have ever experienced. I am guessing if someone soaked you in gasoline and lit you on fire, this is what it would feel like.

The doctor gave me antibiotics and sent me to the optometrist right away to let him start treating my eye. It is scary, and the Shingles have compromised my eye. He is hoping that Prednisone drops will help ward off any damage.

6/12/2014

I came back to Hibbing last night and had to stop by my office at the college today. I ran into Mike Flaten and Steve Rannikar, both good friends and fellow employees. You might think they would have had a little sympathy, but no, nothing but abuse. Mike dropped the *Elephant Man* line on me, "I am not an animal!" Steve hit me with *Terminator* references. They will get theirs someday; right now, I've got nothing.

7/2/2014

Just got home from St. Cloud, MN, tonight. I was able to have the opportunity to coach at the Top 100 Minnesota High School Basketball Showcase the last three days. I have coached the girls' teams the last several years, but this year I was back on the boys' side. Really enjoyed myself.

7/4/2014

Another great 4th of July in Ely. This one was special; at the 1:00 parade, Sheridan Street was packed. There were at least six blocks of filled sidewalks on both sides of the street. The parade was as entertaining as always, and my personal favorites, the Ely Clown Band and the Lawn Chair Brigade, both performed. Pam says when we retire up here she wants to join the Lawn Chair Brigade; I'm all for it. I'll be a groupie. How hard can it be to transport one woman and an old aluminum lawn chair to parades?

We had some family members out to the lake after the parade for a barbecue. Afterwards, nobody else wanted to go into town for the fireworks because it was raining, so I went by myself and enjoyed them immensely.

7/5/2014

I was invited to the Ely High School Class of 1984's reunion at Scotty and Carol Magee's on Burnside Lake. 1983–84 was the one year I taught and coached in Ely and I was honored to be invited to the their 30th reunion.

I enjoyed it immensely, but I still can't believe it has been thirty years. I got caught up with a lot of kids I hadn't seen in years, once again an experience made possible by staying off of Facebook. I ran into Lisa Nelson, an ex-student and younger sister of one of my high school buddies, Mark Nelson. I asked her what she was doing these days and she told me she was a natal nurse somewhere in the Cities. She told me that when she was growing up her dad was the manager of the Ely Hospital and they lived right across the street from the hospital. I knew all this, but what I didn't know was that whenever she was bored she went to the hospital to look at and help with the babies. She established her career choice years ago.

After I got back to the cabin, Pam and I went to the Boathouse and Dee's in Ely to attend some more reunions. The class of 1979 was having theirs and had an open invitation to other classes. Pam is a 1978 graduate and I graduated in 1977 so we both have friends in the class of 1979.

Sometime during the night I ran into an old friend, Ted Loushin. Ted is recently retired and was back in Ely trying to decide his next move. Ted wanted me to play the role of "Wingman" for a while. Pam was busy talking to friends, so I gladly obliged. I did good and introduced him to a couple of interesting women. I am a huge fan of the television show *How I Met Your Mother*, so it was a rush to say; "So, have you met Ted?" Later I did introduce him to a horny divorcee; she was all over Ted. It didn't work out, but I think I might have a future as an occasional wingman for Ted.

7/14/2014

Those Canadians are at it again. They dropped one of those polar vortexes on us again. I'm at the cabin, it is about 11:00 PM, and it is 42 degrees. Minnesota broke several records today for lowest daytime highs on this date. I'm still not believing these global warming theorists!

7/15/2014

I am a baseball guy through and through. I remember the day when I would have given up a body part to see the Major League Baseball All-Star game live. To see any of those players — Willie Mays, Tom Seaver, Jim Palmer, Pete Rose, Johnny Bench, or Brooks Robinson, any of them — all in one game.

Tonight, Minneapolis hosted the All-Star Game at Target Field. My son, Blaine, was at the game and attended the Homerun Derby last night. This is the second time Minnesota has hosted the game since I have lived in Minnesota; the last time was in 1985 at the Metrodome.

I woke up this morning knowing Blaine would be at the game. I was jealous all day long. I watched the first five innings at the Winton Roadhouse; $2 for tap beer and $2 hot dogs while the game was on. I listened to the rest of the game on the radio back at the cabin. WELY broadcasted the game and I sat by a fire and listened. It was perfect!

I am no longer jealous of Blaine or anyone else who was at the game. It entered my mind that these all-stars are Blaine's all-stars, not mine. It seems to me that my true passion for major league baseball was when I was young; now I just spectate, no emotional attachment.

I'll sleep well tonight. It was a great day at Fall Lake in Winton, MN, and there was no post-game traffic.

7/16/2014

Caught a couple of walleyes on Fall Lake tonight. It is about time; my hope was beginning to dwindle. Finally, I'm at the cabin and have enough fish to grill for supper. Great day!

7/19/2014

Stacked two loads of wood, stained two of the garages, and I'm starting to feel somewhat normal. My bout with shingles finally might be coming to an end. There is still some numbness and tingling above my right eye, but I am feeling a lot better.

7/20/2014

I was writing some notes and ran out of ink in my last pen from the C'mon Inn in Thief River Falls, MN. I'll have to steal/borrow a few more this fall when we go there for volleyball. They have always been my favorite pens, always worked well and wrote smoothly. I have terrible penmanship, but the C'mon Inn pens always seemed to help.

7/24/2014

Pam and I had a big breakthrough in our employer and employee relationship this week. On Tuesday she headed up to the cabin and left me here to take care of the Bed & Breakfast alone, a huge deal on her part. Granted she only left me with five guests to take care of and I only had to cook breakfast for two of them for two days. On the first day I cooked an egg & sausage scrambler over hash browns and on the second day I did blueberry pancakes and bacon. I also did fruit and yogurt plates and made coffee and juice. I urged the guests to complain to Pam, because I don't want a promotion. They were reluctant and actually complimentary, but I hope word that I did okay doesn't get back to Pam. I am perfectly happy being the groundskeeper. The other guests, I just had to check-in and ask them every once in a while if everything was okay or if they needed anything.

I don't know how Pam does it; I found that just a little bit of inn keeping was stressful. I didn't have to take reservations, clean bedrooms or bathrooms, do laundry, or make beds. She does this all the time and sometimes we have 14 to 16 people staying with us. Like I said, I don't know how she does it! I am glad she trusted me to take over for a couple of days so she could get up to the cabin; she deserves and needs time away.

7/25/2014

I have had this written in my notes for several weeks now and I need to get it typed in before I lose it.

I have coached and taught high school and college student-athletes for 33 years now. Every season one of the major goals is to establish a solid and positive team chemistry. Whether it happens or not always determines the level of success in a given season.

To establish that chemistry, I am always trying to figure out what draws the kids together outside of the sport. Once I can figure out the various things that draw them to each other, the next step is to establish goals that we all agree to. Those goals unify a team throughout the season. Outside of the season, those goals don't always exist and you start to see these kids separate and drift apart.

What I have noticed over the years is that the things that draw them together are the same things that cause points of contention and separation. Kids are drawn together by school, music, sports, financial situations, work, Facebook, the internet, conflicts with parents and family, religion, and interpersonal relationships, just to name a few. They also find their niches based on decisions and choices they make concerning sexual relations, drug and alcohol use, partying, and boyfriends/girlfriends.

The sharing of these common interests, events, and issues tends to bond and unify kids in positive and negative ways. When they enter into an activity that provides specific goals to achieve, they are able to set personal concerns aside for common goals and focus on those, at least the kids that buy in.

When the activity ends, or sometimes even when it is in progress, those personal issues tend to divide them. I really haven't been able to figure out why they can't step back and realize that what is causing rifts in their relationships is really what drew them together to begin with. Also, none of their social problems are quite as big as they want to believe they are. It really does come down to what we believe to be true at the time. Our perception is — for good or bad — reality, which may not always be a pure truth.

It is always difficult watching these kids go through these growing pains in their young lives. You hope and pray they will work their way through it and come out okay on the other end. You do everything you can to help, advise, and guide them, but they have to do the work. I think the most important thing they need to learn and deal with is that everything they say or do impacts others, positively and negatively. Nobody can exist without impacting or being impacted by others.

8/2/2014

Summer session grades are complete; we have at least two sophomores who will not be academically eligible to participate in men's basketball for the fall semester. Life will go on, but it is always a major disappointment when this happens. I hope we have some incoming freshmen ready to step up and take care of business.

8/3/2014

My mom and sisters, Lisa and Terri, all came up and stayed at the lake this weekend. I think they all understand now why Pam and I are so excited about having a place on Fall Lake. I'm sure they will all be back.

8/8/2014

For all practical purposes, my summer came to a close today. Volleyball practice starts on August 10th, so after today I won't be getting back to the lake anytime soon. I am going back to Hibbing tonight.

After getting some work done this morning, I decided to get a little fishing in. I had four leeches left and couldn't let those go to waste. It came down to the last leech, but it was worth the wait. I finally caught a good-sized walleye on Fall Lake. Twenty-three inches; I was excited and got my cell phone out to take a picture. In the process, the fish flopped in the boat and I fumbled my phone and dropped it in the lake. It is now at the bottom of the lake in about twenty-five feet of water. My identity and contacts should be safe.

Not a complete loss; I got a new cell phone right away tonight, I saved the fish, and Pam and I ate it.

8/17/2014

We have had one week of volleyball practice, and we might just have a play-off caliber team. If this group of young women continue to mature and learn to practice and play like "Big Girls," I think we'll get there.

Yesterday we scrimmaged the alumni in the morning. It is always fun to see ex-players and get caught up. After the scrimmage I headed straight to the lake. My time there will be limited this fall, so I am going for every day I can get.

Last night I went to the Long Branch in Winton to catch the end of the Blues Fest Concert. I had a great time and a very special non-Facebook encounter. I ran into Dave Gotchnik, a friend since high school that I, or anyone else, rarely get to see. Dave is a great guy but pretty much a social recluse. Dave, like myself, is a Blues fan and it should not have been a surprise to see him there. Anyway, it just capped off a great day to see him and visit for a while and listen to some great music.

Life in Winton has its simple pleasures and I look forward to spending more time there in the years to come.

8/22/2014

Great day; my volleyball team and I are in Fergus Falls, MN. We scrimmaged Minnesota State today and play in their tournament tomorrow to open the 2014 season. After the scrimmage, we made our annual team bonding trip to Barnesville, MN, to attend the Potato Days Festival. Four of our players participated in the Mashed Potato Wrestling and represented Cardinal Volleyball very well.

I'm still not sure if this will be my last trip to Potato Days with one of my volleyball teams or not. I'm still contemplating retirement.

8/25/2014

We played well on Saturday. We still have to settle in on a line-up, but I am convinced this season will go well if we stay healthy. Conference play starts on Wednesday at Itasca CC. We were supposed to play Fond Du Lac on Tuesday, but they have decided to forfeit their season due to lack of numbers.

Fond Du lac TCC entered our league a few years ago and have always struggled to field women's athletic teams, but this is the first time in volleyball. I know their coaches work hard to recruit and assemble teams and I feel bad for them. I really feel bad for the student-athletes that don't manage to experience a great time playing in our league and at this level. You only have so many years in your life to play competitive athletics, and I think it is a shame for anyone good enough to have the privilege to play to miss out or pass on the opportunity.

After the Itasca match, we travel to Saint Cloud and Saint Paul, MN, to play in triangular tournaments on Thursday and Friday. I wish I could remember who the "Stupid Man" was that scheduled three straight days and five matches in a row on the road. Oh yeah, it was me! I hope we can play through it.

8/29/2014

We got back from our volleyball trip and I am heading up to the lake. Pam, my son, a couple of his friends, and my daughter and son-in-law are already up their waiting for me. Who am I kidding? It is Labor Day weekend and they are already there. I am just excited we are all going to be there and sharing time at the lake.

9/2/2014

The weekend was great. When I do next year's volleyball schedule, I am going to make sure the whole Labor Day weekend is open.

Most of my career I have looked at Labor Day weekend as a great time to get a couple extra volleyball matches in. The experience with family and friends this weekend has changed my perspective. Labor Day weekend will now stay reserved for a last summer hurrah at the lake. I hope I am around long enough to share it with family and friends for several years to come.

9/4/2014

I was recently reading through the Obituaries in the Duluth News Tribune. I do this on a routine basis in all newspapers I read. It is not out of morbid curiosity; I just like reading the brief recap of people's lives.

There was one obituary in particular that caught my attention.

The obituary was in reference to a man who had died at the age of forty-two. The obituary stated that he had died of natural causes. If we have an average lifespan of well over seventy years old, then how can someone die of natural causes at forty-two? There is nothing natural about that. I know this is a phrase used quite often to describe a death, but what does it really mean?

I wonder about mysteries such as this on a daily basis. Should I be worried? I have also been wondering how long gluten has been in food and exactly when some people became allergic to it.

12/26/2014

Day after Christmas. This was one of those years when our kids were not home for the holidays. Kind of takes the shine off of things. Lexie and Jeff stayed in Nebraska with Jeff's family, and Blaine did Christmas with Alex's family. Big news over the holidays, Blaine and Alex got engaged and will be getting married in June of 2016, on the 25th I think, so I will still be able to make the College World Series next year.

It has been a while since I last wrote. Just wanted to say that volleyball went well. We started to play like "Big Girls" as the season progressed, finished fourth in the conference, and qualified for the post-season. We lost to Central Lakes in the Region semi-final. All in all, a good season. Christina Wickingson and Ebony Gray ended up with All-Conference, All-State, and All-Region awards, and Christina will be an Academic-All American. It was good to be back in post-season play and next year's team should be able to make even a deeper run.

We are well into the basketball season, and it looks like we will only lose one player to academic ineligibility over the holiday break; this is a good thing at the JUCO level. We return to practice January 2nd. I have been enjoying coaching men's basketball again, but I really hope we can start playing smarter when conference play starts.

1/5/2015

Pam and I went to the TRA (Teachers' Retirement Association) office in St. Paul today to get my retirement questions straightened out. Things look too good to pass up, Pam is on board, and we are going forward with it. After the TRA meeting, we did some "Pam" time and went to Bauer Brothers and Architectural Antiques to look at cabinets for the cabin. Perfect side trip; Pam got to look at a lot of stuff and didn't buy anything. I do think Pam was a little disappointed, though, because we didn't run into Nicole Curtis from the HGTV show Rehab Addict. Apparently she frequents both places.

1/7/2015

I don't know about the rest of you, but on occasion GEICO radio commercials get into my head. The one I have been losing sleep over lately is the one that asks about pants and why they are called a pair of pants and you only get one. If you dare, give it some thought. Pair of socks (2), pair of shoes (2), pair of aces (2), pair of pants (?).

1/16/2015

Finalized my retirement plans today, yay!

1/17/2015

We played basketball at Northland TCC today in Thief River Falls; we lost 84–62. I am glad I won't have to make this trip three or four times a year anymore. I'm tired of being homered in baseball, basketball, and volleyball and having to spend eight hours traveling to do it. A few years down the road I might miss it; I have always loved the challenge of playing there.

5/31/2015

I'm sitting at the kitchen table in the cabin. Felt like writing. I'll eventually get to a computer and check when the last time was that I made an entry in what might be book number three. Right now I am at the lake and off the grid, just the way I like it. I'll see if I can use up the ink in my Winton Roadhouse pen and jot down a few thoughts. It is not like I haven't been thinking, I just haven't had the motivation to write down any thoughts in what has probably been months.

First I want to confess that I kind of stole my Winton Road-house pen, but if it helps me get around to writing another book,

I'll learn to live with the guilt. I usually try to keep the pen if I use a charge card to pay for dinner.

I am not sure, but I think my last entry was in January, so let's get caught up. Has anyone figured out why it is called a pair of pants? Big decision here: should I go back to January or work back from today?

January and February went by quickly. As I mentioned before, I did decide to enter into a semi-retirement. So this was my last year of coaching basketball. I was blessed enough to coach for thirty-four years, all as a head coach. Twelve years of high school and twenty-two of college ball. My high school years were split between Lake Park (5 years), Wadena-Deer Creek (5 years), Ely, and Norwood-Young America (1 year each), all in Minnesota. My college years were divided between Brainerd, MN (Central Lakes College/ 4 years) and Hibbing CC (18 years). I coached boys' and men's basketball for 27 years and women's basketball for seven years. This year I went back to coaching men's basketball after spending the previous seven years coaching the women.

This season was full of twisted emotions. My men's team was stocked with a great bunch of young men. Three sophomores and seven freshmen. As far as wins and losses go, it was not the best year I have experienced, but I enjoyed going to work with these guys every day. Two of our three sophomores have committed to four-year schools for next year. Anthony Fisher is headed to the University of Minnesota-Morris and Beau Howard will be at the College of St. Scholastica in Duluth next year. Both are very deserving, and it is always a good feeling to see our student-athletes graduate and move on to play elsewhere.

The women's team, coached by Kate Brau, had a great year. They finished second in the conference and went on to Regional play. Kate did a great job coaching those ladies; I knew she would. I admit, though, it was tough to watch a team that had several players I had either coached the year before or recruited, but I was glad to see them succeed under Kate's leadership. Christina Wickingson is moving on to play basketball and softball at Bethany Lutheran College in Mankato, MN, next year. They are getting a great kid and she will do fine there.

My wife and son were in attendance at our last home game. It was great to have them there despite the anticlimactic loss to Vermilion. A couple of weeks later I coached my last game at Central Lakes College. We got kicked big time, but a few of my ex-players showed up and we visited afterward. I don't know what the final score was; I just know we got drilled. I do know that I spent the last several minutes of the game having career flashbacks flow through my head. I don't know how it works when you die, but I hope it is the same. I had nothing but great memories rapidly flowing through my mind. If that is the way it goes when you die, I can't think of a better way to go, as long as it is the highlights of your life that flash back.

So that chapter of my life, as far as I can tell, is over. My college coaching career of twenty-two years started and ended in the Central Lakes College gym. A rich and blessed circle of life completed. I'm still not sure why they call it the "Circle of Life" when there are so many twists and turns that are taken throughout the journey.

I am also left to wonder: if you start in one place and end in that same place, have you accomplished anything and did you really go anywhere? I am here to tell you the answer is yes! Those twenty-two years were made up of over 260 players, 520 games, 13 states, hundreds of thousands of practice minutes, and countless miles and hotels. I can never thank the people I have shared this journey with enough.

I plan to continue to coach volleyball and teach a few classes at Hibbing CC indefinitely. How long is really up to administration. I have to admit I have a hard time not being "Coach T" to someone. I'll cross that bridge when it comes.

On paper, my official semi-retirement date was May 19, 2015. Please don't tell the state of Minnesota, but this is a great gig. I start collecting my pension in June (tomorrow) and this fall I will still be coaching volleyball and teaching the same classes I have been teaching. The state will continue to pay me and my insurance in addition to my pension. That will happen for the next two years and I will ask for an extension. If the extension is not granted, that will be the end of the run, but I will be paid for one full-time year without being able to work for the state. I'm not making this up; it is called the Annuitant Employment Program. The state of Minnesota came up with this so anyone qualifying for the Rule of 90 (age + years of work) would consider retiring to save the state some money. Yeah, I don't get it either, but it works for me.

I think my wife likes the arrangement; I will work less, get paid more, but won't be at home bugging her yet! The bottom line is that I am kind of retired and loving life. I am still a "Stupid Man," but life is good and I am only a few weeks away from becoming "Grandpa Mike," and I am at the lake jotting down "Random Thoughts." Speaking of which, did you know that on July 17, 2015, Disneyland will be sixty years old? The gates first opened in 1955 for those of you that are mathematically challenged. I haven't been there since 1972, and I don't know what holds true today, but in 1955 the adult admission was $1 and it cost 25 cents to park a car at Disneyland. You can't even park in Canal Park in Duluth for fifteen minutes for $1.25.

Basketball ended in February, and I am proud to say we hired a new coach in late March. His name is Tim Routheaux and he's from Ironwood, MI. Tim is the son of Deke Routheaux, who coached forever at Gogebic CC in Ironwood. Deke retired a few years ago, and I always enjoyed coaching against him. Tim will do a good job and I hope he is here a long time. I also hope he appreciates coaching at Hibbing CC and feels as blessed as I did to have had the opportunity to coach here.

Enough about the coaching or the absence of; as I said before, life is great. My daughter will be giving birth to our first grandchild in a few weeks, and my son is engaged and will be getting married next summer. My mom is doing well, Pam's mom and dad are doing okay, and I am at the lake enjoying the view through a new window, drinking a glass of wine, and jotting down "Random Thoughts." If that is not enough, to top that off, I'll be in Omaha in two weeks to watch the College World Series. Today is a great day to have a great day!

6/1/2015

[12:05 AM] I'm going to bed; Good talk!

9:12 PM [Still June 1st]

First today and then I am going back to try to catch up. Good day today; Larry Urbas showed up around 8:30 this morning to work on re-siding the cabin wall which we put a new window into a couple of weeks ago. I really enjoy working with Larry. He is our contractor at the cabin, but more importantly he's a high school classmate. We weren't close in school, but I think we are building a pretty good friendship spending all this time working on the remodel on the cabin. I am a little jealous, though, that my wife pays him and I get nothing. Admittedly, though, he is the skilled labor and I am just the grunt.

I bought lunch for us today. It is hard to beat that $5 lunch basket at Dairy Queen. After Larry left, I had a quick dinner (hot dogs, for those of you who care). Actually, they were turkey dogs. My son's fiancé, Alex, who is a dietician, left them here last week. She is trying to get all of us to try healthier eating alternatives. These were pretty good, but I am still not ready for tofu or kale.

After dinner I headed to the big city (Ely). I went to Shopko and bought some grass seed and a $4.99 DVD with 25 old western movies on it. We still don't have any television at the cabin so I am hooked on old westerns and Magnum PI DVD's. Night time entertainment at the cabin pretty much comes down to DVD's, Twins baseball on the radio, a campfire by the lake, reading or a short bike ride to the Winton Roadhouse to watch a game. I try to keep my options open. Tonight was a bonus night, my nephew Logan and cousin's son Brock had a little league game, so I watched that for a while. Ely only has four little league teams so it is pretty much a given that one of them has a game or two every week. Tonight I heard the players cheering on a kid named Beckett. I heard them yell his name several times. I don't know Beckett, but I liked hearing the name yelled out at a game. Lexie and Jeff plan to name our grandson Beckett. I had to call Lexie and tell her I hope they don't change their mind about the name. It is a great roster name: Beckett Baack.

Remember I am off the grid for the most part when I am at the cabin, but I did hear on the radio that Bruce Jenner is now Kaitlin Jenner. I apologize if I misspelled Kaitlin; give me a little slack, I heard it on the radio. He also said that every day he lived as Bruce was a lie. I'm just going to put this out there: I have a signed copy of a picture of Bruce celebrating his Gold Medal at the 1976 Olympics. That is the truth and I might be willing to sell it.

The Twins got rained out tonight, so that rules out that entertainment option. I am going to have to decide between an old western movie or reading; oh, the stress of cabin life! We'll see how the rest of the season goes, but let it be duly noted that on June 1st the Twins are in first place of the American Central Division.

I promise when I get back to writing I'll get this book caught up. I don't know about you, but I never really enjoy books or movies that jump back and forth; it confuses me. If there are any "Stupid Men" reading this, hang with me; I'll get there. If you see me before I get there, keep me there—I'll be there soon.

6/5/2015

Okay, let's do this. Reader's Digest version January 2015 until today. For those of you not familiar with the Reader's Digest, I'm doing a condensed version.

IMMEDIATE FAMILY: My son, Blaine, is engaged to be married June of 2016. His fiancé, Alex (Alexandra), is from Becker, MN. They have lived together a little over a year now. Blaine and Alex came to the cabin last week and did their engagement pictures at Kawishiwi Falls on Fall Lake. Blaine turned 30 in April. We went to Chicago in March to celebrate his birthday and my semi-retirement. We stayed at the Congress Plaza on Michigan Avenue. Nice place with a lot of history; it's supposedly haunted, but we saw nothing to back that up. We went to the first three days of the Big Ten men's basketball tournament—good time. We also did our own walking tour of Chicago. We went to the Chicago Sports Museum . . . very disappointing. Ate a lot of delicious pizza during the week. I hope Blaine enjoyed the trip. I know it goes down in my book as some special father-son time.

Lexie turned 32 in May and is pregnant with our first grandchild. She is due on July 3rd, but her doctor expects her to go about two weeks early. We already know the baby is a boy. Lexie and Jeff plan to name him Beckett Michael Baack. I love the name and am honored they have chosen Michael as the middle name. For now, we just pray every night that mother and child both come through healthy. I am really looking forward to this grandpa gig. Pam and I are going to Nebraska next week so Pam can help Lexie out. I was going down for the college world series as usual, but now with Lexie possibly having the baby early Pam wants to get down there ASAP.

Pam has been her amazing multi-tasking self, running the bed and breakfast and supervising Larry and I, keeping the remodeling projects on track. She and her mother had a huge rummage sale in Ely last week. I know she is anxious to get to her daughter. We were talking about it the other night and she started crying. As usual this "Stupid Man" was confused. I thought it was a good thing she would be there before, during, and after the birth. She agreed but said she was crying because she was remembering how hard it was for her not having her mother there when our kids were born. She remembered every detail, including her thoughts and feelings at the time. I'm not going to lie; I know I was there, but most of it is a blur.

JOB: As I said before, I am now officially semi-retired and loving it. Volleyball practice starts August 9th and school starts the end of August. Maybe semi-retired is the wrong terminology; let's say semi-employed.

FAMILY: On Memorial Day weekend, my youngest sister Stacie and her family came to the cabin, as did my Uncle Lynn and

Aunt Kathy. Classic family weekend at the lake. We went fishing, canoeing, had a barbecue, and a couple of nights of campfires. Luckily my nephew Jadon caught a Walleye on his last catch so he can take that off his bucket list. This was probably the longest amount of time Pam and I have spent with Stacie and Jeff's kids. They have only lived in Minnesota a few years. Jadon and Britney are twins and are in the 9th grade; Jack is five. They are moving back to California in a few weeks, so it was a blessing to have this time together. I hope they can get back here again in the not-so-distant future. I think Jeff and the kids would want to, but I'm not so sure about Stacie— it might be a little too outdoorsy for her. I hope she enjoyed her time here, but she wouldn't use the outhouse and I think she may have gotten the shakes if she had to go a couple of more days without Starbucks Coffee.

My oldest sister, Terri, gave us all great news. She is selling her house in Austin, MN, and buying a condominium. The whole family is excited for her; it will make her life so much easier. A person her age and with her physical ailments has no business taking care of a house all by herself. Terri prays more than any of us, but this time all of our prayers have been answered.

My sister, Lisa, and her husband, Mark, are soon to be empty nesters. My niece, Bethany, graduated from UW-Madison this spring and has taken a job with Cargill in Minneapolis. My nephew, Grant, graduated from Wayzata H.S. and will be attending UW-Madison this fall. They are great kids, but I want Lisa and Mark to know they are going to love empty nesting; I know Pam and I do.

My mom is doing pretty good. I know she still lives with a lot of pain, but she has been doing well. I say this with caution because she has taken a fall the past two years when I was at the College World Series. That streak has to end this year because Lexie could be having the baby during that time also. I have put my request in with Lexie to wait until after June 16th to have the baby. I have tickets for the first four days of the CWS. Omaha is only a little over an hour from the hospital, but I hope Beckett and Lexie can cooperate.

THE CABIN: New window is in, and the kitchen is gutted and awaiting remodel. We bought the lakeshore across the road from the cabin so we now officially have a lake cabin, but don't tell the IRS. Projects are now on hold until the baby is born and Pam and I get back from Nebraska.

FRIENDS: Tough couple of weeks. I was a pallbearer at Bill Wirtanen's funeral. Bill, several years my elder, is an ex-coach and athletic director at Mesabi Range Community College in Virginia,

MN. Over the years he became a beloved friend and mentor. Bill died after a long bout with cancer. I still can't figure out why the family asked me to be a pallbearer, but I was honored. Bill was what every coach, teacher, husband, and grandfather should aspire to be. The Mesabi Daily News called me to comment about his passing; the word I wanted to emphasize was "integrity." I hope that came across in the article.

This past week, Kurt Zuidmulder died of a heart attack at a baseball practice at Hermantown High School. I knew Kurt as a good friend and colleague at Hibbing Community College. Kurt was our football coach until 2006. Despite high blood pressure, it is ironic that at 48 Kurt died of a heart attack. He had one of the biggest hearts of anyone I have known. Kurt may have died young, but he didn't cheat life; he lived it to its fullest.

Okay; we are all caught up now. Nice day today — it finally stopped raining. Now the mosquitos are all fired up! I got four new tires put on my truck today. Had some time to kill while they were working on the tires at Tony's so I played tourist in Ely. Went to breakfast at the Taste of Ely. If you haven't been there in a while, the menu has changed. The Lake One is now the Chapman Street breakfast. Don't ask me why. It is still the same great breakfast. After breakfast, I browsed through a few shops. I bought a bib, pajamas, water shoes, and a couple of books for Beckett. The books are also for Pam; they are *Good Morning Loon* and *Boundary Waters ABC's*. Pam will love the first book because morning is her favorite time at the lake.

The stores I went to in Ely today were doing pretty well. Seems to be a lot of tourists in town today. It must be frustrating for shop owners who count on the summer season to make or break them every year. I bought the books at Legacy Toys. I really hope Beckett can spend some summers here because I need an excuse to spend more time shopping in there. I picked up the bib and pajamas at Ely Wear and T-Shirt Shop. I saved the best for last; I found the water shoes at the Ely Surplus Store. If asked, I would tell you that the Ely Surplus Store and L&M in Hibbing are by far my favorite stores. If Beckett is a really big kid he can wear the water shoes when he comes to the lake next summer; if not, he can wait until he is about three years old.

I was a true tourist in the other shops I went into; I looked at everything, thanked the owners, and left without buying anything. I call that scouting for Christmas. On the way out of town, I stopped at Skube's Bait Shop and picked up some Chubs and Leeches. This equaled two perch and a marvelous afternoon of fishing on Fall

Lake. I'm not in Wisconsin or North Dakota so no excitement over the Perch but the weather and the scenery were fantastic.

11:26 PM: In case you are keeping tabs or my wife asks, I did not go to the Roadhouse tonight. I had a fire by the lake. Now I'm going to bed to read until I fall asleep. Life is good!

6/8/2015

10:40 PM: Just got back to the cabin. I went to the Roadhouse to have dinner and watch the Blackhawks vs. Lightning Game 3 of the Stanley Cup Finals. A large family from Chicago was in the bar to watch the game. They are camping at Fall Lake Campground and don't have television either. Turns out they have been coming to Ely for over 35 years, three generations. One of the Uncles attended Bemidji State University, as did I. He played football with Toot Anderson and Terry Vessel, both guys from Ely that I know well. The Grandma has also written two books. More proof of how if you just take the time to visit with people the large circle of life can be reduced to small, intimate circles.

I won a $1.50 tonight on quarter bets. Fifty cents that the winning team would have three or more goals and one dollar that the winning goal would be scored by a player wearing an odd number. Usually I do my quarter betting with Connor, a bartender at the Roadhouse, but tonight was special; I also took money from two of the grandchildren of the Chicago family. I did feel guilty when I found out they had borrowed their quarters from their grandma.

I was back in Hibbing Saturday to do some yardwork. Sunday I came back to the cabin, planted my tomatoes, and went fishing. I actually caught dinner for the first time this summer. Two really nice Crappies. Still hoping for my first Walleye catch this year, but the Crappies grilled up just fine.

Big news this weekend was Pam's announcing that she is ready to sell our bed and breakfast and move to the lake. That is huge. Hopefully it is not long before it sells. We have had the B&B for over eleven years and I think she is starting to burn out, loves the lake home, and I'm sure wants to create more flexibility in our schedule to get to Nebraska and see our grandson more often. Plus, Blaine and Alex will be married next summer and living near the Twin Cities, and we think more grandchildren are coming not too far into the future. I don't really know where the future will lead us, but somehow we'll blend Ely, the Twin Cities, and Nebraska into our lives. If we had it all figured out, things would not be as exciting as they are. I like where we are headed.

Seriously, if it all works out, I think we are blessed to only be in our mid- to late-50s and we are able to move into this phase of our lives; semi-retired/employed and grandparents. I just hope the price of gas doesn't go up too much.

I'm slowing down. It took me five hours today to weed wack and mow our property at the lake. I hope there is a riding mower in my future.

After I got done mowing, I went to the Fat Chicken Greenhouse in Winton and bought another tomato plant, cage, and t-shirt. I am a t-shirt guy, always looking for unique ones. The Fat Chicken is a Greenhouse and Nursery and also houses the Winton, MN, U.S. Post Office; top that for unique.

I tried to call my mom today and left her a message that I would call back. I'm overdue for calling her, and I know she'll point that out to me. She could call me also, but that counterpoint never flies with her.

6/12/2015

Pam and I are celebrating our 33rd wedding anniversary today. Big to do: we went to Sportsmen's Café for breakfast. I gave Pam a card and a new audiobook to listen to on our trip to Nebraska. She gave me a bottle of cologne. After all that hoopla, Pam did laundry, got rooms ready for guests checking in tonight, and went grocery shopping. I took care of some things at my office, went to Valvoline to get the truck ready for the trip, and then came home and cut the grass. We topped all that off by loading the truck with all the wonderful baby stuff we have to take to Lexie. I finished the evening by packing my suitcase. We plan to leave about 6:00 AM tomorrow morning, stop at my sister Stacie's to pick up a changing table for the baby, and then stop at my nephew Grant's graduation party and then on to Nebraska. Should be a great day, he says tongue in cheek. The pay-off: quality family time in the Twin Cities and a ten-hour drive to Auburn, NE. What keeps this all in perspective is that I know I'll be at the College World Series in Omaha on Sunday afternoon. This is obviously a "Stupid Man's" version of a baseball junket.

Yesterday I had serious doubts as to whether or not Pam and I were going to make it to 33 years. A few days ago she closed out on some Do-Bid auction items from an old school in Bovey, MN, once a high school and most recently a middle school in the Greenway school system. She won bids on three cabinets and two doors. The catch: you had to come take them out yourself. I am not talking just carry them out; the buyer was responsible for doing the demolition work to remove them. These were not wall mounted cabinets—they were built into the walls. Yesterday was the day, and they had to be out of the building by 5:00 PM. They are beautiful oak cabinets and doors built into the school in the 1920s. You quickly get over the beautiful part as the task of removal begins. We got over there about 9:30 AM and returned to Hibbing with the last load at about 9:00 PM. Pam came up with the wonderful idea to buy two more cabinets while we were there. They will look great whenever we get around to installing them in the kitchen in the cabin. Larry is going to love this project. They will look fabulous, I'm sure, but it will be only Pam, me, and the two guys we paid to help us who will know how much work it took to get those things out of that school. Thank God those two guys showed up, or we would have never gotten them on our own and Pam may have gone missing in Bovey.

This event leaves me with something my mother-in-law says on occasion: "Aren't you glad you married that girl?" The answer is still yes and always will be, but I am glad my mother-in-law wasn't there to ask me at about 6:00 last night.

Off to Nebraska; I'll check in again with you in a few days.

6/16/2015

Nothing new on the baby watch. I'm still in Omaha at the CWS. Arkansas and California State Fullerton are not; both teams have been eliminated, two and barbecue.

Good day t-shirt shopping; eliminated teams drop to half price in the vendor tents in the baseball village, so I picked up a "Hog Pile" and a "Clash of the Titans" shirt. I also picked up a t-shirt for Mike Flaten—don't tell him it was off the $5.00 rack.

Pam and I got to Auburn, NE, on Saturday night. Unfortunately we didn't lose anything off the pick-up load we brought to Lexie and Jeff. We brought a changing table and crib hardware from my sister Stacie, a bookshelf, and enough miscellaneous baby stuff and clothes from my mom, sister Lisa, other relatives, and Pam and I to last Beckett for the next three years. My sister, Terri, sent my boyhood rocking chair, which had been in her attic for some unknown reason. All this along with our luggage for two weeks.

No baby yet. I should feel guilty; I'm at the CWS for the third day and Lexie, Jeff, and Pam have been working on getting the nursery ready. I'll pitch in tomorrow and Thursday. Friday I'll go back to Omaha and watch the semi-finals.

Vanderbilt won the suspended game this morning with a walk-off homerun. This afternoon I visited with Karl Ellison, the Vanderbilt catcher, out in the bleachers. Real nice kid; very humble. His parents should be proud. He was sitting by himself until I took it upon myself to strike up a conversation. He said he came out there to get some junk food from the concession stands and just be a fan for a while.

The Vanderbilt vs. TCU game starts in about an hour. "Go Dores!" I have to stop writing now; I am taking notes on my menu and people are starting to stare.

6/17/2015

Lexie and Pam went to Lincoln today for Lexie's last appointment before the baby is born. I went back to Omaha and watched Florida beat Miami. Breaks my heart to see Miami get eliminated (sarcasm). Lexie's appointment went well, and if she doesn't go into labor over the weekend, the doctor will start inducing her on Monday night and Beckett will be born on Tuesday.

6/18/2015

I didn't go to the game today; I stayed at Lexie and Jeff's. I put the ceiling fan up in the nursery and stained the bookshelf. The ceiling fan works, but of course it is a little noisy, so hopefully someone with a skill set better than mine will remedy that in the future. At the end of the day we went to Tarkio, MO, and looked at two houses. No apparent reason other than Lexie and Pam's curiosity. We came back to Auburn and had dinner with Jeff's parents, Jim and Ginny.

Tomorrow I'm going back to the CWS to watch the semi-finals and on Saturday we should be able to move the furniture into the nursery. Hopefully Sunday will be a day of rest for everyone to await the birth of Beckett.

6/21/2015

8:30 PM; Nice Fathers' Day. Still no grandson. So much for a day of rest; it turned into move-in day for the nursery. Jeff and I finished the quarter-round trim for the nursery. I finished staining the bookshelves. Not my best work, but it will have to do. Pam and Lexie have been trying to finish final decorating touches. There will still be more to finish tomorrow.

We grilled outside tonight but had to eat inside. Lexie, Jeff, and I thought it was okay to eat outside, but Pam is melting in the Nebraska summer heat, so we dined in. Tomorrow is ground zero. Lexie and Pam have a few things to finish in the morning. Jeff will go to work most of the day, and I am heading back to Omaha at 2:30 to watch Virginia and Vanderbilt start the championship series of the CWS. Vanderbilt won last year over Virginia. It is intriguing to see the same two teams back in the finals again. This year Virginia is kind of a Cinderella Story. Dustin Pleshe, an ex-baseball player of mine, is driving over from Des Moines to meet me at the game. Haven't seen him for a couple of years and I'm looking forward to seeing him again. Another great non-Facebook moment. Lexie and Jeff are going to the hospital in Lincoln around 6:00 PM. The doctor will start the inducing process later in the night and hopefully Beckett is born sometime Tuesday morning. This all getting very exciting. We'll see how it all plays out, but Beckett should be born on Tuesday, June 23rd, and a whole new set of parents, grandparents, great-grandparents, uncles, and aunts will be created. I know it sounds sappy, but I can hardly wait.

6/22/2015

Lexie and Jeff went to Lincoln tonight to check into the hospital. Pam and I will drive over to Lincoln in the morning. Vanderbilt opened with a win over Virginia tonight. Dustin met me before the game. I bought the tickets; he bought dinner. Dustin is doing great; he will be moving to Florida in August for a construction business venture. If you have read my other books, you may remember that Dustin was in my first book under "Dumpster Diving." To say the least, Dustin has had an interesting journey over his twenty-eight years. He seems to have his life on track, and I am proud of him. These kind of stories are why I cherish my years of coaching. I can't begin to explain how good it feels when you see your ex-players turn out to be successful adults. It's very much like being a proud parent.

Tonight, I will hit my knees and pray one more time for the good health of Lexie and Beckett and as smooth a delivery as possible.

6/23/2015

The baby watch is over! Lexie gave birth to Beckett Michael Baack at 3:51 PM today. A healthy seven-pound, twenty-inch baby boy. Lexie, Jeff, and Beckett worked through about a seven-hour labor while Pam and I anxiously hung out in the waiting room. All I can say is "Praise God!" Beckett is a beautiful, healthy baby and Lexie is doing great. All prayers are answered. I can't really put it in words, but holding Beckett for the first time was amazing. It was joy in its purest sense. I really hope Pam and I can be a big part of his life and we find a way to close the gap between Minnesota and Nebraska—and I'm not talking about Skype or Face Time.

6/25/2015

Lexie and Jeff brought Beckett home today. Pam and I will stay here until Saturday morning and then drive back to Minnesota. We are looking forward to going home, but it is already very evident that it is going to be hard to leave Beckett. It is going to break Pam's heart, and I am not real sure how well "Grandpa Mike" is going to handle it, either.

Side note: When Pam and I drove back to Auburn from Lincoln this morning, we drove by a steakhouse outside of Syracuse, NE, that was, according to the sign, "The Home of the Testicle Festival." It was not open but I had to stop and take a couple of pictures. I swear every time I go to Nebraska I see something I have never seen before.

6/28/2015

Pam and I got back to Hibbing about 11:00 last night. The trip took about 17 hours. We stopped in Glenwood to make some arrangements for Blaine and Alex's wedding for next summer and then stopped in Perham to see Jean and Paul Weinzerl's cabin. We did get to see Lexie, Jeff, and Beckett in the morning before we left. Pam handled it very well. I did notice on the way home, though, that she spent a lot of time looking at pictures of Beckett on her phone and tablet. Hopefully they can get up to Minnesota Labor Day weekend. Two months is about all we will be able to take, waiting to see them again.

I am not going to lie; I thought it was the hardest thing we ever did when we left Lexie at college her first year. That was gut wrenching but pales in comparison to leaving your first grandchild, daughter, and son-in-law. I know all will be well, but at the same time, this was hard. I cried a little and tried to not let Pam see; I didn't want her anymore upset than she was.

Caught up on some newspaper reading today. Kudos to the Supreme Court on lifting all remaining state bans on Gay Marriage. To steal one from Colin Cowherd, "Bout Time!"

7/7/2015

Fourth of July weekend at Fall Lake and in Ely was fabulous. Blaine and Alex and four of their friends were up all weekend. Pam and I enjoyed having them here but were both worn out when everyone went home. Blaine and I are staying at the cabin this week; Pam went home on Monday.

On July 3rd we watched two fireworks displays on the lake. Saturday night, Pam and I went out in the boat and watched Makis' fireworks and were also able to see the city fireworks in Ely at the same time. I love fireworks and can never get too much. The parade in Ely was great as usual; the Lawn Chair Brigade and the Ely Klown Band were my favorite highlights. Special year on the Mayor's float: Ragnar (Minnesota Vikings' Mascot) and Medusa, the ex-professional wrestler, made guest appearances. I get Raganar (Joe Juranitch), he is from Winton, but I don't know what the Medusa connection is.

We barbecued on Saturday with family and friends. Extra treat: Blaine's friend Steve did the grilling—day-off for me. These kinds of gatherings at the cabin are special. Pam's dad, Rodney, was there, and I hope he realizes none of this would be possible without his support in allowing Pam and I to buy the lake property.

Almost forgot; big event at the Winton Roadhouse on Friday night. The first ever reunion for anyone born in the Winton hospital. Pam, Mike, and Diana Petrich, Bob and Ann Marolt, and I all went. Diana was the only one of us born in Winton, but the rest of us made it past the bouncer. We were all able to bask in Diana's glory—good time! Saturday we also participated in the somewhat-annual Fall Lake Flotilla. Petrichs picked us up in their pontoon and we cruised the lake.

Larry has been here the past two days and Blaine and I helped him finish remodeling the "Bunkhouse." Just in time for Blaine's bachelor party this weekend.

I need to sleep well the next few nights because I know Blaine's guests are going to cut into my sleep time. I hope all goes well.

I know it will be way too late by the time you read this, but I hope you all voted for Brian Dozier, the Twins' second basemen, to make the All-Star team. I appreciate the passion and support the Kansas City fans have for their Royals, but they have turned the All-Star balloting into a mockery. Major League baseball needs to revisit the balloting process before next season.

7/8/2015

Really didn't think I'd be writing tonight, but Pat Surface inspired me. Blaine and I went back to Hibbing for the day and got some work done at the house. I'm sure Pam wished we had done more, but the yard looks a lot better. We got back to the lake around 6:00. We brought back three cabinets for the kitchen in the cabin, some of the cabinets Pam and I took out of the old Bovey High School.

Pat Surface and his wife Donna did an outdoor concert in the parking lot at the Winton Roadhouse parking lot. They call it "Wednesday Nights in Winton." I always enjoy seeing and hearing them perform. Pat plays guitar and sings; Donna does a little singing and signs many of the songs. Pat does Northwood's folk songs. If you haven't heard them, check out his music sometime. He does a great job of capturing the Northwood's (End of the Road) feeling. I would call tonight's performance more of a friendly gathering at the Roadhouse. Things had to end by 9:00 because there is some kind of Winton city ordinance against a gathering outside like that after 9:00 PM. Anyway, they will be there for the next several weeks and I really hope Pam and I can go together next week.

Speaking of Pam, she should be able to get up here again on Monday. It is also her birthday that day (July 13th); don't let me forget. I spaced it out once years ago and that didn't go over real well.

Today there was a smoky haze in the air again. We are blaming those damn Canadians again. It is not bad enough when they send those polar vortexes down here in the winter; they also have to send us forest fire smoke in the summer.

I'll get over the smoky haze soon enough, but it will be a while before the Bill Cosby stuff is forgotten. I remember buying his comedy albums, watching the cartoons, and reading his books and later watching the Cosby Show on television. I would like to believe that Cliff Huxtable would have never drugged and forced himself on women. In addition, being born in Philadelphia and living a large part of my childhood in that area, and knowing he was a Temple University graduate, put him in a special place in my mind and heart. Now with all the allegations about drugging and raping women, if true, he is on my list of scumbags. I wouldn't say I idolized him, but it was close. He has definitely fallen from grace. My dad, who I did idolize, died in 1989. I always did idolize him and he has never let me down. I hope my son can say the same thing about me after I have passed.

Speaking of dying, in my first book "Random Thoughts of a Stupid Man," I mentioned I want to be cremated when I die. I also listed places I want my ashes to be scattered. Pitcher's mound, the left hand batters' box, and over the right field fence at the Ely Memorial Baseball field. The pitcher's mound at the Bemidji State University baseball field. The Hibbing Community College gym floor and off the deck of the Pink Pony Pub in Gulf Shores, Alabama. I would also like to add under the apple tree in the backyard at our house in Hibbing and on Fall Lake, off the dock, would be okay, and maybe by Lovers' Island. Whatever is left of my ashes can be put in a jar and put in the same gravesite with Pam in a plot in the Ely cemetery. I'm sure I will die before Pam, so she can take care of this.

I also just noticed looking through my first two books that I numbered the random thoughts; sorry for not doing that this time. I guess this book is more of an account of daily random thoughts.

7/12/2015

1:30 PM: I'm going to take a few notes before I take a, well-deserved, nap. I'm here at the cabin all by myself and loving the tranquility of it. My son had his bachelor party here for the past 3½ days. It started Thursday night and the last guests left at about 11:00 this morning.

My son is 30 years old and all the guys were around that age, give or take a year or two. I think there were about 18 or so in attendance. They partied, grilled, pontooned, and played several lawn games, all drinking related, of course. I just basically guarded the property, grilled, kept track of the fire, and cleaned up a lot. I am whipped; three nights up until three in the morning and waking up at 7:30 AM took it out of me.

I think a good time was had by all. Great bunch of kids. I guess I shouldn't call them kids anymore; great bunch of guys. As far as the ones I've seen grow up, it was interesting to hear them talk of wives, children, and jobs. I also got a kick out of listening to some of them call back to their wives and telling them how they were hardly drinking and getting to bed early because they were so worn out from the day's activities. What happens in Winton, stays in Winton I guess!

By my count, nobody got hurt, the cops never had to come by, there was no property damage, and nobody puked where I had to clean it up. Plenty of noise, but how do you get 18 "Stupid Men" to be quiet? We have three neighbors fairly close; two of them had no complaints and one had a meltdown when it was all over with. I guess two out of three would have to be considered a success.

I did tell my son he'd better get this marriage thing right, because there will be no future bachelor parties here.

7/18/2015

Volleyball practice starts three weeks from tomorrow. I'm trying to milk every day at the lake that I can. This week has been a good one. On Tuesday night, Pam and I went to "Tuesday Night Live" in Ely. We had dinner at Rockwood and listened to the Washboard Road Band—great stuff! "Tuesday Night Live" happens for most of the summer in Ely, and it is a lot of fun. Several of the restaurants in town host live music outside and there is a Farmers' Market in Whiteside Park.

We ran into Mike Portugue and his wife at Rockwood. Mike graduated from Grand Rapids High School in 1978. He was an outstanding three-sport athlete: football, basketball, and track. I played one year of basketball with him at Vermilion Community College in Ely. He dated one of Pam's best friends for a while. We don't really know his wife, but she seemed very nice. They live in Lakeville, MN, and have a cabin on Cedar Lake outside of Ely. Anyway, another great non-Facebook moment. It had been several years since we had last seen Mike, at his dad's funeral. Nice to catch up, and we hope to see them again soon.

On Wednesday night, Pam and I went to "Wednesday Night in Winton." Pat and Donna Surface performed again. I look forward to hearing them any time I get the chance. Love their music and storytelling. I have to go again next week because I have stumped the musician two weeks in a row now. I have requested "Who's Gonna Feed Them Hogs" by Tom T. Hall. Pat says he is still working on it.

It hasn't been all fun and games at the lake. I did get the grass cut, and I've been pulling nails from the trim for the reclaimed cabinets that are going in the cabin kitchen. I have also been tearing out the three layers of linoleum floor in the kitchen so we can get back to the hardwood floor. It is coming along slow but sure. I think this is the third time now I have told Pam that I will never tear up a kitchen floor again. The first time was in Wadena about twenty-five years ago. The second time was in Hibbing about fifteen years ago and now this one. I really hope she listens this time because I think a fourth might kill me.

Quick tip if you ever have to refinish an old hardwood floor and remove linoleum or laminate first. Dawn dish soap mixed in warm water and poured on the floor does a great job of softening the tarpaper and glue and makes it a lot easier to scrape off. Also a wallpaper steamer is a great accessory for this job. There you go; I bet you never saw a DIY tip coming in this book!

Friday night, Pam and I went to Sir G's for dinner. Sir G's is Ely's not-so-well-kept secret: fabulous Italian restaurant and great pizza. Pam and I went there on our first serious date in 1976 when it was located across the street next to Zaverls' Bar. We topped off the evening with a relaxing Canoe ride on the lake and up the river. It was a great night, and I think the Deer Flies have finally given up — I hope.

Tomorrow I will work on the floor some more, but I also hope to get out and do a little fishing. Haven't been out for about a week. It has rained a few times and it is a pain in the butt taking the cover off the boat and putting it back on every time. Note to Pam: How nice would it be to have a boat lift with a canopy? Just something to add to the wish list.

I did get to see a replay of Caitlin Jenner's speech at the ESPYS. Inspiring message and she looked fantastic. I realize she is probably taking fashion tips from the Kardashians, but I was not enamored with the Botox-enhanced lips. Never have been a fan of Botox lips, but who am I to judge.

7/20/2015

Didn't get to go fishing yesterday, but it will happen sometime. I did finish getting the rest of the flooring off. Now I just have to work on the tar and glue; like I said before, slow but sure. Today I drove down to Duluth to watch my nephew Grant golf in the State Amateur Championship. The event was held at the North-land Country Club. I walked the back nine with my sister Lisa and watched Grant golf. The course is beautiful and the views of

Lake Superior are immaculate. The weather was fantastic, and it was nice to spend time visiting with my sister. Grant didn't have his best day golfing, but it was still fun to watch him compete. He didn't make the cut but he will be playing in the State Open Tournament next weekend. I hope that goes better for him, and I hope he takes pride in knowing that he has to be good to qualify for these two prestigious events. I don't do much golfing and have limited knowledge of the sport, but I do understand it to be a fickle game. Case in point, Tiger Woods.

7/26/2015

My niece, Bethany, and two of her friends came up from the Cities for the weekend. I think Bethany is hooked on the Ely area. They got here Friday night and left this morning (Sunday) at 7:00 to go to the north shore of Lake Superior. Quick trip, but they canoed, hiked, swam, went to the Blueberry Arts Festival in Ely, and we had a fire on Friday and Saturday night. They also went to Sir G's for dinner. I think they all had a good time. A few things that I have read lately that caught my interest: In a Parade Magazine poll, when poll takers were asked what they would want more of, 30% responded sleep as opposed to 26% which responded sex. 34% chose lose 15 pounds and only 9% chose get a raise as their first choice.

The Americans with Disabilities Act was passed into law twenty-five years ago today. It seems as though the lives of people with disabilities have improved immensely, but I know we have a long way to go. Especially with access to buildings and the use of sidewalks and especially in the winter here in the northland. I also wish people would be a lot more respectful of handicap parking spots.

The Star Tribune ran an article about Kepler-452B, an older, bigger cousin to Earth that circles a Sun much like our own, which was discovered by astronomers. It is about 6 billion years old and we don't know if it contains water. I still get excited thinking about life out there in other solar systems.

8/3/2015

Monday 7:30 AM
This is it; the last week of summer for all practical purposes. Volleyball practice starts this Sunday. I'm sitting in the waiting room at the hospital in Maple Grove, MN. I came down to the Cit-

ies yesterday to stay at my mom's and visit. This morning I brought her to her doctor's appointment. She was scheduled for two heart tests. Hopefully just a routine matter, but she is 80.

We had a good day visiting yesterday. We ran a few errands and sorted out a few things in her condominium. Found some great pictures of my dad from his Navy days that she let me keep.

Saturday night I was in St. Cloud for a Pacesetter Coaches' event. I was presented with a plaque for my 34 years of basketball coaching and 32 years of doing camps for Pacesetter. Definitely not necessary but very nice all the same. Pat Dewey, who recently retired as the Athletic Director at East Central High School and has served Pacesetter for 36 years, was also presented a plaque. Tracey Haines, who has been the Pacesetter secretary for 25 years, was also recognized. I'm honored to be associated with these two in any manner.

Tonight I'll go back to the lake. My sister, Lisa, and nephew, Grant, are coming up for a couple of days. I haven't had Grant out fishing since he was a little kid and in a month he will be a freshman at UW-Madison. I'm really looking forward to it.

On Thursday, Pam and I are going to my Aunt Margie's funeral in Superior, WI. She passed away last week. Margie was my dad's only sister, four years younger. My uncle Lynn and Uncle John are still living on the Turnbull side. My dad and Lynn's twin, Uncle Dick, have already passed. I will always remember my Aunt Margie as one of the most compassionate, optimistic, and genuine people I have ever known. Even when she was sick, she still seemed to have the deepest concern for everyone else. I never look forward to funerals, but it will be nice to see some family members from the Turnbull side who I haven't seen in a while.

I have a ticket for Pat and Donna Surfaces' musical on Friday night. I also hope to play two more days of Pickle Ball this week. I have my own paddle now; I bought one in St. Cloud on Saturday. In between, I plan to knock out a couple of projects at the cabin; who am I kidding? Saturday, I'll go back to Hibbing to finish getting ready for the first day of volleyball.

I am really looking forward to the volleyball season. On paper it looks like a great team. The potential is there for a post-season run if we come together and stay healthy. We had 14 recruits, but it is looking like we'll start with 12. One of my sophomores decided to go to Cosmetology School and another player might not be eligible.

Note to self: Pick up some floating jig heads for fishing this week.

8/5/2015

All I can say is, I am blessed! Lisa and Grant got to the lake around 8:30 PM Monday night. We had a fire by the lake and visited for a while.

On Tuesday, they went canoeing early in the morning and stopped at the Kawishiwi Falls. When they got back, we went to Ely and had breakfast at Britton's Café. Afterwards, Grant and I went fishing until 4:00. The three of us went to "Tuesday Night Live" in Ely. We spent some time at the Farmers' Market in Whiteside Park and went to The Taste of Ely and had dinner and listened to Germaine and Rich, a marvelous folk music duo.

This morning I cooked up my infamous "Fall Lake Scrambler" for breakfast (sausage and scrambled eggs over hash browns). I am not sure about Lisa, but I think Grant was impressed. After breakfast I went to town and played Pickle Ball for two hours while Lisa and Grant hiked the Bass Lake trail off of the Echo Trail road. Grant and I fished for three hours in the afternoon, and Lisa stayed at the cabin and read, napped, and swam. Fishing was slow, the lake was as smooth as glass, and the weather was fantastic — great afternoon.

Lisa and Grant left about 3 o'clock. I went into Ely and got a haircut. I couldn't find a barber open, so I ended up at the Haircut Shop, which is pretty much a salon. They did a good job, and also trimmed my eyebrows and ears. I'll find out tomorrow if Pam approves.

I don't know if she notices my haircuts, but she always notices if my eyebrows, ear hairs, or nose hairs need to be taken care of. Afterwards, I cut some grass and then went to the Winton Roadhouse to have dinner and listen to Pat and Linda Surface. Today was the last time I'll see them perform this summer. I'm sure I will experience some minor depression next Wednesday when I can't attend "Wednesday Night in Winton." I really hope the Roadhouse brings Pat and Linda back next year.

Today was nearly perfect. I say nearly because Pam was in Hibbing. Don't tell her I said this, but, like the line in the Jerry McGuire movie, "She completes me." I really do look forward to getting the B&B sold and completing my personal retirement so we can spend a lot more time in the same place. It will definitely be an adjustment from our current lifestyle, but it will be good.

I hope Lisa and Grant went home recharged. Lisa will be back to teaching and Grant will be off to college soon. I hope they left with full hearts after spending a little time at the "End of the Road."

It is a great place to slow down and even stop for a while. We want everyone to feel welcome to visit.

I heard on the radio today that Pierce Brosnan (ex-James Bond) was detained in an airport somewhere because of a knife he was carrying. That happened to me years ago in Hawaii. It was in my shaving kit; I used it to peel oranges. I don't think that incident made the national news. I don't know all the details on Pierce, but it must have been a slow news day.

I stopped and talked to Karl Rukavina today to see if he has been getting the cherry tomatoes I have been leaving on his porch. He said he has and has been loving them. He told me he eats a salad every night and always includes the tomatoes. I can't eat the tomatoes fast enough, so I'm glad he is enjoying them.

8/6/2015

Today was a good day for the wrong reason. I know at various times we tell people to "Have a good day" or a "great day!" Today the advice should have been, "Have the day you have."

Pam and I drove down to my Aunt Margie's memorial service in Poplar, WI. It turned out to be a wonderful day celebrating the life of a truly beautiful and genuine person. Her obituary read:

Marjorie Clausen, age 78, passed away peacefully on the evening of July, 31, 2015. She was surrounded by her family at the time of her passing. Marjorie is survived by her husband of 55 years, Kenneth Clausen, daughter Pauline Schroeder and sons Kenny and Marty Clausen. Brothers Lynn and John Turnbull.

Margie was born in Hibbing, MN, on July 9, 1937. She was the second child of Herbert and Effie Turnbull and sister to Jack, Lynn, Dick, and John Turnbull. Margie grew up in Poole Location in Northern Minnesota; she worked in a hardware store in Hibbing while helping raise her younger brothers. After college she moved to St. Paul, MN, and worked as a secretary for the president of Minnesota Fence and Ironworks. She met Ken at a camping retreat and it was love at first sight. Margie and Ken moved to California and raised their family for thirty years before moving to Wisconsin.

Margie loved the outdoors and made numerous camping and boating trips. She adored square dancing, spending time with friends, and taking care of others. Her true passion was her family; she idolized her children and grandchildren and found great joy in following their achievements.

Margie was a kind, gentle woman with the biggest heart and was loved by all for her compassion and thoughtfulness.

There was a small pamphlet handed out at the service, titled, "A life remembered." I want to share two excerpts; the author was not given.

When I come to the end of the day and the sun has set for me, I want no rites in a gloom-filled room.

Why cry for a soul set free? Miss me a little, but not too long and not with your head bowed low. Remember the love we once shared.

Miss me, but let me go. For this is a journey we all must take and each must go alone. It is all part of the Maker's plan, a step on the road to home.

When you are lonely and sick at heart, go to the friends we know and bury your sorrows in doing good deeds. ~ Miss me, but let me go. ~

The second excerpt was a poem titled "The Dash" by Linda El-lis. I'm sure many of you have read it before, but if not, please take the time to check it out; very inspirational! Puts a great spin on how lives should be led and judged.

As I said earlier, today was a good day for the wrong reason. A very special person has left this earth, but I and all the others who knew Margie can celebrate because she is at rest and peace in a bet-ter place. We are all better people because Margie was in our lives. It was a blessing to have friends and family come together today and honor her.

My family will celebrate Christmas this year as usual. We will decorate the tree and I will place a drum (an ornament my Aunt Margie sent to me in third grade) on the tree as I always do, but this year the ornament is moving to the top of the tree. Aunt Margie, I will try to let go but I will miss you.

8/7/2015

For all practical purposes, today was pretty much my last full day to spend at the lake this summer. I'll be going back to Hibbing tomorrow to pump up the balls, set up the net, and get ready for our opening day of volleyball on Sunday. I'm a little disappointed to be wrapping up the summer, but I am excited to start a new vol-leyball season. I really like the team we have coming in this year.

So I know you are on pins and needles wondering how I spent today. I woke up around 8:00, had a couple of muffins for breakfast, and went into Ely and played Pickle Ball. I came home and started tearing down another wall in the kitchen at the cabin. Mike, Eric, and Pat stopped by to move the piano out of the living room. We are giving it to the Magees. This is good because the piano used to belong to Carol Magee's grandma and it was left here when we bought the cabin. We bought the cabin from Leona Hayes, Carol's grandma. I finished the wall after those guys left. I went to Ely and returned some sand paper to Ace Hardware and stopped into Ely Wear and picked up birthday presents for my niece and nephews. Britney and Jadon had July birthdays and Jack's is in September, so August fits. I came home, cut the grass down by the lake, and had supper. After that I went to the Vermilion Community College Theater and watched Pat and Donna Surface's Musical, "Remember When," and loved it. It was also a fundraiser for combating Alzheimer's disease—great cause. If you want to contribute, go to spiritwoodfoundation.com. After the musical, I stopped at the Winton Roadhouse and had a Surly. Too crowded in there tonight, so I went home. There is a Water Cross event tomorrow at the Long Branch so a lot of racers were at the bar.

I know by the time you read this it might be too late, but go see a Water Cross race sometime. It is a snowmobile race on open lake water. This year Hairball, a heavy metal tribute band, is in Winton tomorrow night. Take my word for it: Winton, MN, is a happening place!

I capped off the evening by putting more Citristrip on the kitchen floor. I'll let it sit overnight and see if I can scrape the floor some more in the morning.

Now, I'll quit taking notes and go to bed and read until I fall asleep. I just heard a commercial on WELY, the Ely radio station; it said, "Ely is one of the two greatest places in the world and they haven't discovered the other one yet." I'll put my vote in for Winton (Fall Lake).

8/16/2015

The first week of volleyball practice went very well. We started practicing last Sunday and capped off the week with a five-team round robin scrimmage at Mesabi Range. On Saturday we scrimmaged our alumni. Both scrimmages went well. Friday we were pretty sharp for this early in the season. We still need to work hard on improving our communication, especially on defense.

About sixteen alums showed up for the scrimmage, ranging from 2000: my first team at Hibbing CC to last year's team. Sarah Merhar was our oldest alum and Kailey Wirtanen our youngest. I always enjoy seeing the alumni come back and play. I have been blessed to have coached a lot of outstanding young ladies over the years.

After the scrimmage, I headed straight to the lake. I arrived at the cabin around 3:30. I picked up brush that was left after Minnesota Power cut down a couple of trees that were threatening the power lines. I also began shoveling some of the gravel out of the lake and putting it back on the shoreline. A lot of sand and gravel got washed into the lake during a big storm last week. After I was done, I took a bath in the lake and headed to the Winton Roadhouse for dinner and to listen to Earl Bulinski and the Roadhouse Jam Band. I also dropped off more tomatoes for Karli Rukavina.

I left the Roadhouse about 9:00 and walked over to the Blues Fest at the Long Branch. There are only a couple of street lights in Winton, so I was able to see a wonderful display of northern lights (Aurora Borealis) in the night sky on the walk over to the Long Branch. When I got to the gate, nobody was working the entrance so I was able to enter for free — bonus!

I had the pleasure of my annual Dave Gotchnik sighting. Second year in a row now that I have seen Dave (Red Man) at the Blues Fest; otherwise I never see him. I also arrived in time to see the headline band from Memphis, TN. I left about 11:30 and walked back to the cabin. More northern lights and an unbelievable sky of stars afterward. It was really nice out still, so I sat by the lake and took in God's show in the sky and listened to Blues Music for another hour or so. It is really easy to hear the bands playing at the Long Branch from our cabin. Another great night in Winton, MN!

Today I finished the brush pick up and did some more shoveling by the lake. I cut the grass and spent a couple hours in the lake moving rocks and some old dock cribbing. Pretty tired tonight, so I'm not going out; I've got a date with a good book.

Tomorrow I'll play a little Pickle Ball in the morning and then go back to Hibbing for volleyball practice. I'm just glad I was able to get a little time back at the lake, since I probably won't get back until Labor Day weekend.

Grandpa Mike and Beckett, his new fishing partner

Blaine & Alex Engagement Picture
(Photo by Abby King)

Big turnout for Wednesday Nights in Winton
(Photo by Joany Haag)

2014 Hibbing CC Volleyball celebrating play-off clinching win against Mesabi
L-R: Ebony Gray, Emily Hall, Christina Wickingson, Josie Greenwood, Kailey Wirtanen
and Khai LaBarge
(Photo by Nancy McKenzie)

Mike Turnbull

2015 Hibbing sophomores signing day! L-R Beau Howard [Men's Basketball to St. Scholastica]
Christina Wickingson [Women's Basketball & Softball to Bethany Lutheran] and Anthony Fisher
[Men's Basketball to UM-Morris]
PROUD DAY IN CARDINAL COUNTRY!
(Photo by Gary Giombetti)

Grammy Pammy & Beckett June 23, 2015

2014-15 Hibbing CC Men's Basketball: My last Men's Basketball Team
L-R: Dillon Bruns, Mo Abdillahi, Seric Walker, Kioshi Demning,
Markis Watkins, Anthomy Fisher,
Beau Howard, Noah Davis, Antonio Carr, and Denzel Jones
(Photo by Don Monroe)

The view from my favorite seats in TD Ameritrade Park;
2015 College World Series 2015

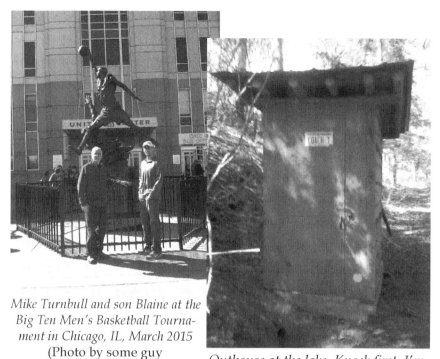

Mike Turnbull and son Blaine at the Big Ten Men's Basketball Tournament in Chicago, IL, March 2015 (Photo by some guy who passed by)

Outhouse at the lake. Knock first, I'm probably in there reading!

Front entrance to the Winton Roadhouse. I usually use the side door. (Photo by Joany Haag)

Beckett's Baptism October 2015
L-R: Grammy Pammy, Lexie, Beckett, Jeff, and Grandpa Mike
(Photo by Blaine Turnbull)

Testicle Festival Syracuse, NE. I'm going someday when
it is actually happening!
(Photo by Pam Turnbull)

Hibbing CC Volleyball 2014 : Played like "Big Girls."
Front L-R: Khai LaBarge,Christina Wickingson, Sydney Lough
Mid L-R: Emily Hall and Kathryn Wojiechowski
Back L-R: Kailey Wirtanen, Ebony Gray, Ellen Lescarbeau,Gabby Sund-
quist and Josie Greenwood
(Photo by Larry Ryan)

2015 Hibbing CC Volleyball at Fergus Falls Tournament
Front L-R: Sydney Lough, Michelle paulsen, Alex Cromley, Sam
Wardas, and Miranda Wickman
Mid L: Emily Hall
Top L-R: Zoe Bystrom, CJ Jesperson, Ashley Mossuto, and Khai LaBarge

Winton Point Aerial View over Fall Lake: The grassy area by the shoreline is our property.
(Photo by Mike Turnbull while flying with Bill Hill)

Kawishiwi Falls on Fall Lake
(Photo by Alex Crapser)

*Pat and Donna Surface performing at the Winton Roadhouse. That is
Connor manning the Tikki Bar*
(Photo by Joany Haag)

New windows at the cabin. Great view of the lake.

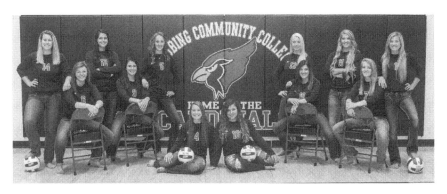

2015 Hibbing CC Volleyball
L-R: Ashley Mossuto, Michelle Paulsen, Sam wardas, Zoe Bystrom,
Emily Hall, Stydney Lough
Khai LaBarge, Kathryn Wojciechowski, CJ Jesperson, Alex Cromley,
Elizabeth Eccles, and Mirand Wickman
(Photo by Larry Ryan)

Alex & Blaine: Another bachelor goes down!

Beckett [R] & Edwin [L], best friends at daycare.
(Photo by Lexie Baack)

Fall Lake sunset.

Shingles! Day#3
(The only selfie I have ever taken)

The Fat Chicken:
Winton, MN Feed-
store, nursery, and
U.S. Post Office.
(Photo by Pam
Turnbull)

Fall Lake view from new windows in cabin kitchen.

8/17/2015

Played Pickle Ball this morning, probably last time until next spring. I'll miss it. I've really enjoyed the times I've played; it's a great bunch of people to be around and they have been very helpful teaching me the game. After Pickle Ball I drove back to Hibbing and dropped off my niece and nephew (Morgan and Logan) at their mom's house in Chisholm.

When I got back to the college, I picked up the meal money check for tomorrow's scrimmage at Central Lakes College in Brainerd. I went to the bank to cash the check and witnessed what might be the rudest thing I've ever seen someone do. I was sitting at the drive-thru with my window down. The lady in the lane next to me rolled down her passenger side window and dumped her ashtray. The ashes blew into my window. I looked at her and said, "Really?" She mumbled something, took a draw on her cigarette, and flicked her ash. I looked at the ashes and butts on the ground, looked at her, and again said, "Really?" She mumbled again and rolled up her window. Definitely not one of Hibbing's finest.

Tomorrow we travel to Brainerd for an 8-team scrimmage, another chance to see if we are getting closer to playing like "Big Girls."

8/18/2015

Good trip to Brainerd for volleyball today. Played pretty well and ate at Mickey's (my favorite sub sandwich restaurant). Alex still isn't healed from ankle injury but hopefully will be by the weekend. We did make it from Hibbing to Brainerd and back without making any potty stops. Anyone who has coached women knows that is a big deal!

8/21/2015

Sitting in my hotel room in Fergus Falls; we have a team meeting at 9:00 in the lobby. Hopefully the team is back from Applebee's by then. We play a four-match tournament tomorrow to open the regular season. We will be short three players, but I am still expecting a good start to the season.

On the way down here we listened to XM radio in the van. I noticed there were HD stations. I get HD television, better picture, but how does HD apply to radio? I drive a 2004 Ford F-150; what other technology don't I have?

I introduced the freshmen in my van to the "Movie Game." Sam needs work! 8:55, so I have to get to that meeting.

9/2/2015

First of all, the Fergus Falls Tournament: We went 1 and 3, a slower start than I anticipated, but I still have no doubt that we will improve quickly and eventually compete for a play-off spot. Last weekend we opened our conference season with home matches against Fond Du Lac and Itasca. We split: defeated Fond Du Lac 3-0 and lost to Itasca 0-3. We were very sharp on Friday and easily took out Fond Du Lac. On Saturday we made way too many errors (serving, ball handling, and communication) to defeat a team like Itasca. It is always a learning experience for young college players to learn to play back to back on a weekend and remain consistent.

We started classes on August 24th. I love the beginning of a new school year; students and staff are always fresh and excited. It is just a good vibe on campus. I have been teaching and coaching for 34 years now and I still get wrapped up in the anticipation of a new school year. I am glad I have a job that is full of fresh starts. New years, new semesters, new classes, new seasons, new teams, new students, etc. Change is a welcomed challenge.

Last Sunday I got back to the lake, just for the day. Khai La-Barge, one of my volleyball players, gave me a sign at the beginning of the season. It says, "Today is a perfect day to have a perfect day!" Last Sunday was one of those days. I got all the grass cut, picked up fallen branches, picked tomatoes, and killed a squirrel. That squirrel had it coming; it has been eating some of my tomatoes and it is always a good day when you eliminate a pesky squirrel. After I finished the work at the cabin, I stopped by Karli Rukavina's and left some more tomatoes. After that I went to the Roadhouse and had dinner and watched the end of the Twins' game. They just might make a run at the second wildcard position yet. After dinner I stopped at my father-in-law's warehouse and picked up several bags of clothes to take to Goodwill in Hibbing. I also stopped in and wished my mother-in-law a happy birthday.

On my way back to Hibbing, I checked my phone for missed calls, and the screen on my phone read: CALL LOG EMPTY; perfect! I also checked my inbox for text messages, and my daughter had sent a video of Beckett, my grandson; perfect!

9/8/2015

Just waiting for Enterprise to drop off our rental vans for to-night's volleyball match at UW-Superior. Thought I'd jot down a few things. So much for that; they are here. I'll get back to you later tonight. [2:00 PM]

9/11/2015

I know I said I'd get back to you on Wednesday, but that night got away from me. Let's get caught up.

We lost our volleyball match to Rainy River in 4 sets. The first sets were awesome; we lost the first one 25–23 and won the second one 25–22. The next two were all Rainy River. It was nice to see the girls step up and compete. Tuesday night, that was not the case at UW-Superior. I was very tempted to leave them in Wisconsin after the match. We just didn't show up to play. Today we are in Roch-ester for a weekend tournament. We need to play well and get into a winning mode before we get back to conference play next week.

I left the hotel this morning and walked downtown. I was on a mission to go to the Barnes & Noble in the old Chateau Theater building. It has always been my favorite bookstore, with a very unique location and lots of history. I'm very disappointed to report it has closed and anybody I asked has heard nothing about plans for something else to go in the building. Barnes & Noble still has a store in the Apache Mall. Doesn't really matter to me; the Chateau Theater was what made it attractive to me.

I did walk through a couple of other shops and wandered the streets for a while. I enjoy the buzz in downtown Rochester in the morning. Things really come to life; with all the office buildings, clinics, and hospitals, there are people all over the place. Starbucks, Caribou, and Dunkin Donuts are all hopping. It has a whole differ-ent vibe than Hibbing or Winton. Don't get me wrong, I'd rather wake-up in Hibbing or Winton, but Rochester is a nice change of pace and it never hurts to change ones' pace now and then.

In one of the shops, I looked at signs with quotes. I didn't buy any, but I did write down a couple I think I'll use on my office door or in the locker room.

#1 Dear Karma,
I have a list of people you forgot!

#2 <u>THINGS TO DO TODAY & TOMORROW</u>
WAKE-UP
KICK ASS
SLEEP
REPEAT

3 <u>RETIREMENT</u>: Half as much pay and twice as much husband.

I can't let this week go without mentioning how special Labor Day weekend was. Blaine and Alex came up from the Cities and my Uncle Lynn and Aunt Kathy also came to the lake. Lexie and Jeff traveled up from Nebraska and brought the most special guest, our grandson Beckett. He is a little over 2 months old now. I'm loving this Grandpa Mike thing. I really hope Pam and I can figure out how to get to Nebraska more in the not too distant future.

We all had a great time at the cabin and other friends and family stopped out also. Beckett did not enjoy his first trip in the boat; he cried most of the time. I really hope this changes in the years to come, because I need a fishing partner.

Public schools opened in Minnesota this week. I'm sure there are lots of parents of young kids who are glad to see that. It had to have been really stressful with summer activities ending in mid-August and Labor Day being so late in the month. Three weeks of kids with nothing to do had to be more than a little stressful.

10:00 PM: Great day in the gym today. We defeated Anoka-Ramsey and Riverland today and played very well. I also completed my annual task of finding the Entertainment Weekly Fall TV Preview Magazine for Pam. Big points and kudos to me!

10/3/2015

It's late at night and I debated writing my thoughts because I may have had one too many beers at the Winton Roadhouse tonight, but the walk back to the cabin has me all freshened up, so what the heck; here we go.

We ended up losing two matches the second day of the Rochester Tournament and went on to lose eleven straight matches over the next couple of weeks. Today we won at Fond Du Lac. Everybody beats Fond Du Lac, but we'll take it; the losing streak has been snapped. The losing streak was bad enough, but the 11th loss in that streak was really hard to stomach. We lost to Vermilion 3-0.

I have coached volleyball at Hibbing for 16 years and that was only our third loss to Vermilion. I'm glad to see that Vermilion is getting better, but we didn't need to help them along! Anyway, we are two games out of a play-off spot going into this week. We play all the teams ahead of us still, so to steal one from the *Dumb & Dumber* movie: "So we still have a chance!"

I've had very mixed emotions about the volleyball season. On one hand, I realize our shortcomings but I still feel we should be right in the mix for a play-off spot. When we play like "Big Girls," we are really good; when we don't, we are really bad. My positive thoughts tell me we will be in the play-offs and my negative thoughts tell me we don't have the tools this year. If I'm still writing in a couple of weeks, I'll tell you how it turns out. The bottom line is: we still have a chance and that is all you can ask for. What we do with the opportunity put before us is up to us.

Tonight I am back at the lake for the first time since Labor Day weekend. I got up here too late tonight to get anything done, so tomorrow (Sunday) is huge. I hope to cut grass, move logs, and fix the railing that Larry knocked down and then go to the Roadhouse to eat some wings and watch the Vikes for a little while. It is cold at the cabin tonight, low 30s; tomorrow it should be in the 50s. I'm sure my wife would hope that I get more done, but the bar is not set very high for this weekend. I hope to be back up here next weekend.

My son Blaine called today to tell me he bought a truck. Blaine bought a 2014 Sierra. I have been shopping trucks for two years now. I drive a 2004 Ford F-150 with about 165,000 miles on it. He is 30 years old. What is wrong with this story? I am jealous!

The moon, clouds, and stars are on fabulous display over Fall Lake tonight. I missed the "blood moon" last week, but this is still impressive.

Earlier this week I received a reminder in the mail that I am definitely older. The "Arthritis Today" Magazine sent me a subscription update reminding me I also qualify for a senior discount. How great is that, arthritis and 55+? Never saw that one coming.

This week has been ugly on a lot of fronts. Lost to Vermilion, 15 million T-Mobile customers were hacked, and the shootings at a community college in Oregon. Right now, looking out the window at the moon and the stars over the lake, none of it seems to matter, but somehow in my twisted thoughts it does.

Pretty quiet at the Roadhouse tonight, just the way I like it. It was just me, Connor (bartender), and Joany and Kirk (owners). We all had plenty of time to just visit. Joany wants me to do a book signing sometime before Christmas. She is calling it "Books & Booze." I'm all in, but it will have to be "Books & Beer" that night.

Okay, I'm done rambling; this is where I stand: 1] Volleyball; play like "Big Girls," and we still have a chance. 2] Cabin; we have to keep knocking out projects; it might be our house in the near future. 3] Wife; I still love her. 4] Son; has a nicer truck than I do. 5] Grandson; growing like crazy, and we'll see him in a couple of weeks for his baptism in Nebraska. 6] Current news; just heard on WELY that the shooter in Oregon was not killed by police, he shot himself — gutless! 7] Hope; I think I'm going on the Spring Baseball trip in March to help coach the pitchers. Still have to see if Pam has other plans. 8] Arthritis; I still have RA! I actually participated in a blocking drill in practice on Thursday, which didn't go so well; a couple of touches and no blocks. 9] Weather; a little above average temperatures, and no rain tomorrow. I have to get some yardwork done.

Like I said when I started writing tonight, possibly one too many Roadhouse Ales. Maybe shouldn't have written down my thoughts, but I'm sticking with it. I need to finish this book and get it to my publisher by next month.

Last thought for the night. Pam has done a great job decorating the cabin. It is still definitely a project in the works, but we could move in permanently anytime if we had to. I hope the house in Hibbing sells soon.

10/4/2015

Great day at the lake today. I got a few things done. I cut the grass, organized a few things, did a dump run to Soudan (only dump in the area open on Sundays), moved some logs, and loaded the truck with stuff to take to Lexie and Jeff in a couple of weeks. When it was all said and done, I walked down to the Roadhouse and had wings and watched the second half of the Vikes' game. I took the trail through the woods and walked the road coming back; beautiful both ways. Fall colors on the walk there and impressive star display on the walk home. I'm not a big wings guy, but Rich does a great job on the Captain Morgan wings. The Vikes lost 23–20 to Denver, but I took Connor for $1 on quarter bets. I came in with $1.50 and walked out with $2.50. Connor is getting harder to fool; he acts like he is not paying attention, but I know he is.

I'll go back to reality tomorrow morning, with class at 9:00 and 12:00 and volleyball practice at 3:10. Big week for volleyball; we play Rainy River on Wednesday and Itasca on Friday. I hope we can step up and play like "Big Girls."

I hope I can finish this book next week and get it off to Jansina at Rivershore Books to publish. For those of you who are counting, that would be three books: *Random Thoughts of a Stupid Man, More Random Thoughts of a Stupid Man,* and *Still a Stupid Man.*

Note to self: Just listened to Luther Dickinson on the radio. I need to find a CD the next time I'm in the Electric Fetus. Possibly North Mississippi All-Stars?

Something I learned today: The Soudan dump does not take credit cards, only checks or punch cards. You can use a credit card at the Soudan Store (the only store in Soudan) to purchase a punch card, and they are open on Sundays. Another tip, the Soudan Store has great gas prices at the pump.

10/6/2015

I got a haircut today — actually I had all of them cut. Pam should be happy; I also had my eyebrows, nose, and ear hairs trimmed. Two reasons for the haircut: 1] half of my players did something to their hair over the weekend, and I had to keep pace. 2] I usually get a haircut when I have something seriously intense coming up in my life. Right now that would be our next three volleyball matches. We play Rainy River tomorrow, Itasca on Friday, and Mesabi next Tuesday. We are two games out of a play-off position right now and all three of these teams are ahead of us, so there's no room for error. We are going to have to bring out our A-game every night if we are to have any chance. We have been looking for everyone to play like "Big Girls" all season, and we haven't quite put that complete performance together yet. This would be the time!

We have had two good practices this week, but a couple of our freshmen still don't seem to get it. You need to bring a positive energy and a work ethic to every practice and every game. It is the only way to get better. I realize part of this comes from lack of confidence. I want them to realize that athletic confidence comes from putting in the work and performing quality repetitions.

When I went to the barber today, I walked by a Hallmark gift shop that had a sign outside that said Halloween is October 31st. Who needed a reminder? Not even this Stupid Man! Isn't Halloween always on the 31st? I hope Christmas or the Fourth of July doesn't sneak up on their customers.

I wonder if Babe Glumack will sleep tonight? Doesn't break my heart, but the Yankees just lost to the Astros in the Wildcard game. Say it with me, Babe: "The Yankees lose, the Yankees lose! Start spreading the word!"

10/9/2015

Our possibility of making the post-season in volleyball ended tonight with a 3–0 loss to Itasca CC. This is getting really old, we lost the Region Championship to Itasca in 2010 and haven't beaten them in a conference match since then. I really hope we manage to knock them off before I retire.

As far as wins and losses go, this has been a tough year. We have a great bunch of kids, but we have struggled with consistency and playing with the confidence and intensity it takes to win at the college level. We refer to it as playing like "Big Girls" or "Playing like you get it." We have struggled all year with getting "It." We have had our moments but no consistency.

I am full bore into recruiting for next year and very hopeful we can turn it around next year. I am down to coaching one sport for the first time in my 35-year career, so next year can't come soon enough. We need more arms, and I have to find players who want to compete every time they step on the court. Some of our freshmen should be solid as sophomores, so I hope most of them return for next year.

I was thinking how easy professional teams have it. If they have a bad year, they are rewarded with a higher pick in the draft. When a college team has a bad year, they have to go out and find players who believe they can come in and make it better next year. This is one of the reasons I love coaching at the college level; it is always a challenge, and you don't get rewarded for mediocrity. I think there are a lot more life lessons in college athletics. In high school you can finish the regular season in dead last and still get a play-off game at the end of the year. How does that teach anyone that you have to compete and you get what you earn?

I drove up to the lake tonight after the match; I hope to get some work done on Saturday and Sunday. Pam is coming up on Sunday.

On the way up, I heard on the radio that some people are protesting President Obama's presence in Oregon today following the shootings. One guy said this is not the time or place to promote his gun control agenda over the bodies of dead children. I tend to disagree. This is the 15th time in Obama's tenure that he has had to address mass shootings in the U.S., be it schools, theaters, or malls. I won't pretend to have the answers concerning gun control or what it would take to stop these incidents, but maybe we need to start listening to anyone that has an idea to stop these mass killings from happening. At this point I really don't care where anyone sits on the gun control issue, but it is pretty obvious something has to be done. We are getting pretty good at killing ourselves. If we can't handle the privilege, the right to bear arms doesn't make much sense. I'm thinking if you can't prove that you are a hunter (animals/wild game) or a trap shooter, there should be no way you can purchase a firearm. Online sales should be banned also. For what they are worth, I guess I do have a few ideas.

10/13/2015

We play Mesabi in volleyball tonight. Normally an outstanding rivalry, but they are a lot better than us this year. They will probably make the play-offs as the number two team, and we are not going to be in the play-offs. Hopefully we step up and play well.

10/14/2015

We lost 3–0 to Mesabi last night. Pam and I are leaving for Nebraska when I'm done with class today. Beckett is getting baptized on Sunday.

10/16/2015

Pam and I and Blaine and Alex got to spend the day taking care of Beckett today. Alex got Beckett to rollover during "Tummy Time." We all agreed not to tell Lexie and Jeff because we don't think they have seen him do this yet. They should be the first. Blaine and Alex got here last night; they are going to be Beckett's Godparents.

10/17/2015

Blaine, Jeff, and I went to Lawrence, KS, today and watched the Kansas vs. Texas Tech football game. I bought the tickets a few weeks ago. Kansas is terrible this year, so I was able to get $70 tickets for half price from a season ticketholder. Row 1, forty-five-yard line, on the Kansas sideline. Kansas played Texas Tech tough and we all enjoyed the game.

I always enjoy getting to come down and visit Lexie and Jeff, but I am not looking forward to a third night on the hide-a-bed in the basement; my back is killing me.

10/18/2015

Great day! Beckett was baptized in a Lutheran church in Auburn, NE, today. First big milestone for our grandson, and we were blessed enough to be there. I hope Lexie and Jeff follow up and raise Beckett with church being a part of their lives.

Blaine and Alex left for home after the Baptism, so I will still be in the basement tonight, but I'm getting upgraded to a real bed. In case you are wondering, Pam has been upstairs in the guest room every night. Perks of being the grandma, I guess. Pam and I will head home early tomorrow morning.

10/19/2015

Back to reality; we drove ten hours back to Hibbing and had volleyball practice at 8:00 PM. I took my second personal day from work today. Second one in 35 years; still haven't taken a sick day. I know, "Stupid Man."

We play a match against Gogebic CC in Ironwood, MI, tomorrow and then finish with Central Lakes and Northland coming to our place this weekend.

10/23/2015

We lost to Central Lakes tonight. Last game of the season is tomorrow against Northland. As I said before, it has not been a banner year in the win column, but I have a great bunch of kids. They have been a treat to coach, but we have struggled to turn all the hard work into wins. No post-season this year, so I guess I'll be handing out candy on Halloween.

Tonight I met with our sophomores. We gathered in the gym to say our goodbyes. I had four good ones this year: Sydney Lough, Emily Hall, CJ Jesperson, and Khai LaBarge. They have been a joy to coach, and I will have a tough time letting them go tomorrow. We would have had five sophomores but we lost one at the beginning of the year to academic ineligibility.

Mike Turnbull

10/25/2015

The volleyball season ended yesterday and I already feel depressed; no practice on Monday. I look forward to ending the day in the gym with those kids and going to work.

The post-season void is deeper than usual. This is the first time in my career that I am not coaching basketball and rolling from one season to the next. I'll admit, I feel lost. I have always had basketball to jump into right away, usually before the volleyball season is over. I'll have to wait a whole year to make amends for this year. I hope my 2016 team will be as ready as I will to get to work.

Now I have to focus on recruiting. We need everything. We are graduating two Defensive-Specialists, a Setter, and a Middle Hitter. Hopefully recruiting goes well and we get the right freshmen back. We have been to the post-season eight times and have missed it eight times, and personally I like being in the post-season a lot better. I plan to go recruiting at the Minnesota State Volleyball tournament in a few weeks. That will be the first time since 1998, since basketball has usually kept me away. I'm looking forward to it. I have only been to the tournament three times: twice as a coach with my Wadena-Deer Creek teams and once as a parent to watch my daughter. This will be my first time for recruiting purposes.

10/30/2015

Dodged a bullet today. Pam, her mom, and I looked at the old Winton Post Office with a realtor. It is being sold for $25,000. Pam wanted to buy it for retail space and rooms to rent. Luckily it is a pit and should be demolished. There is a tin ceiling in there, though, that we would love to have.

11/1/2015

I am going to close out this book in the next few days but not before I comment on an article I read in the paper a couple of weeks ago. You'll just have to be patient; I'm gathering my thoughts.

11/3/2015

I apologize to those of you who have been waiting two days to hear what I have to say about that article. I'm still working on it.

Today, I did experience one of the perks of not coaching basketball. It was about 60 degrees and sunny, a rare occasion in early November in northern Minnesota. I was able to rake leaves all afternoon and take them to the city compost pile. I'll call that a bonus day without basketball practice.

When I was out in the yard raking, kids started walking by at about 3:00 after school let out. Apparently I can add "old creepy guy" to my profile. A girl was walking down the sidewalk toward me — I'd say she was probably a ninth or tenth grader, not that it matters. When she got to the corner by our house, she put her cell phone to her ear, I assumed to avoid any conversation with me. As she passed by, I heard her say, "Nothing, I just wanted to talk to someone until I got past this old creepy guy standing in his yard." I said, "I heard that. You could have at least said, 'old creepy guy raking leaves' or at the least, 'old guy.'" I'm not going to lie; the "creepy" comment kind of stung. It left me thinking that it was only 35 years ago that I was the "hot, young, new teacher at the school," according to those same-aged girls. I don't want to know when I turned into the "old creepy guy"!

I'll try to find time to get back to that article tomorrow; right now it is time to watch "The Voice" on television. I guess that is what us "old creepy" guys do. I am sure I am not the only "Stupid Man" who does. I do have my pride though; I still don't watch "Dancing with the Stars."

11/5/2015

My daughter, Lexie, is the head volleyball coach at Auburn High School in Nebraska. Her team is in the section final against Ashland-Greenwood. The winner goes to the state tournament next week.

I am following the updates on the computer. It has been gut wrenching. Auburn lost the first two sets and won the third set. Every set has been back and forth.

Lexie is in her second year as the coach at Auburn. I know she thought they had a great chance to win this match. My heart goes out to her as a dad and fellow coach. I know she'll be heartbroken if they don't pull it off.

The match just went final; Auburn lost the fourth and final set. I kind of hope she doesn't call tonight to let me know how it went. I'd rather have that conversation after she has had a chance to absorb the loss and come to grips with the outstanding season they had.

I've been a dad for 32 years and I still have a hard time talking to my children on the phone when I know how badly they are hurting. It is always a struggle to say the right thing, if there is a right thing to say. Usually it is better just to listen and let them air it out.

She is doing a great job coaching, and I know she'll get to that state tournament soon.

11/6/2015

Lexie didn't call last night, so I didn't have to try to talk smart. I'm sure we'll talk sometime this weekend.

I'm going up to the lake this weekend. Pam and Blaine are already up there. I have to stop at the eye doctor in Ely for an appointment. It is a follow-up to have my eye checked to make sure no damage has been done from the Shingles I had this past year. The Shingles' rash was very close to my right eye. Dr. Bremner did a great job of treating me. I have also asked for an exam for the purpose of getting glasses. It is time to stop using Readers (Cheaters) from the Dollar Store. I have gone through dozens of them. I have no problem with distance, but anything right in front of my face is becoming more and more difficult to read, and computer screens are the worst. I'm guessing bifocals. Hopefully, Pam will come to the appointment and help me pick out frames, since she is the one that has to look at them.

I guess I will have to talk smart sometime this weekend. Deer hunting season opens in Minnesota tomorrow morning. I don't hunt, but I know I will run into a lot of guys in Ely and Winton who are hunting this weekend. So I have to be on top of the lingo: gauges, points, spreads, pounds, rubs, scrapes, distance, temperature, blinds, stands, upwind, downwind, snow/no snow, permits, buck or doe only, drives, etc. The big trick will be to act like I care!

Blaine is going to hunt with the Petrichs. He is not carrying a gun this year; he is just going with. He'll have to decide for himself if he likes it. I went twice in college and never really got into it, but maybe he will.

Now that I am tuning up on this talking smart thing, maybe by Sunday night I can write my thoughts about that article I mentioned and finish this book and get it ready for the publisher. Pam and I have to meet Bud and Becky Ode, dear old friends from Lake Park, in Walker, MN, on Sunday for lunch. If we get back early enough, I'll get it done after I do some school work and make a few recruiting calls.

11/9/2015

All right, let's talk about that article. I read the article about a month ago and it has been in that dark distant place, called the back of my head, ever since.

The article appeared in the Duluth News Tribune on October 12, 2015. It was written by Bob Shaw, a writer for the St. Paul Pioneer Press. The article was titled "Traditional prep sports declining." (Football and hockey are among those on the wane, while lacrosse is on the rise.) Some of the bullet points in the article included:

1] Newly released figures from the National Federation of State High School Associations show participation declines in football, baseball, softball, and both boys' and girls' hockey and basketball.

2] These legacy sports are being dethroned by such upstarts as lacrosse, soccer, and cross country. And a new champion of high school sports has emerged: boys' and girls' track and field, which claims the highest combined total of athletes in Minnesota.

3] Although there are exceptions, many teens are migrating from team sports into more individualized sports.

4] Jody Redman, associate director of the Minnesota State High School League, said that shifts are partly due to the inherent limitations of team sports, which limit the number of athletes who can play. Example: In volleyball, only 6 can play, so you might carry 15 to 16 players. Track and Field is open to as many as can participate.

5] Hockey is slipping. The phrase "Minnesota: State of Hockey" is okay as a chamber of commerce slogan. But it is not exactly accurate any longer. In the past 10 years, participation in girls' hockey has dropped 7%, and it has dropped 12% in boys' hockey. Hockey is now tied with swimming, with about 9,600 boys and girls in each sport.

6] Cost is a contributing factor: Cross country? (Running shoes.) Swimming? (Not a lot of equipment there.) Hockey? (All the equipment and ice time.)

7] For generations, baseball has only been second to football in boys' participation numbers in Minnesota; but no more. Track and Field has overtaken America's pastime.

8] Although football is still the single sport in Minnesota with the most participants, 23,800 boys in 2014–15 school year, the number has dropped 8% since 2004–05.

9] Injury fears are also a contributing factor, especially concussions.

10] Participation Derby:

- Soccer is surging, but basketball is down sharply for boys and girls.
- Wrestling down 6% since 2004–05.
- In swimming it is a split. Boys' swimming is up 27%; girls' swimming lost 17% since 2004–05. Swimming is struggling nationwide, because 1,300 public schools across the country have closed pools in the last 10 years.
- Golf: Plummeting faster in Minnesota than any other sport. Boys' golf down 18% and girls' golf down 16% since 2004–05.
- Lacrosse: Increasing more rapidly in Minnesota than any other state according to the NFSHSA.

I felt that Bob Shaw did a very good job of researching the material for this article, but I was left wanting to interject my off-the-cuff opinion. So here goes. You can take it for what is worth. You can also determine the worth yourself and interject your own opinion.

The safe way to explain the drop off in participation would be to attribute it to declining enrollments at the schools. I'm sure Minnesota isn't the only state that has declining enrollment figures. Smaller families and fewer kids, especially in rural areas. Areas that are gaining in enrollment are growing in ethnicities that don't play some of the legacy sports. Some schools offer more sports to fewer kids than the number of sports they offered years ago when they had more kids. Something has to give.

I also feel that some of the team sports might be declining in participation numbers because it is just easier for kids to participate in individual sports and not have to be accountable to a team. I see more and more kids choosing ease and convenience over hard work, dedication, and commitment to others.

Probably not a popular opinion, but I would also blame homeschooling. It seems to me that the majority of the homeschooled kids I have come in contact with participate in individual sports if any at all.

I also believe you can't underestimate the impact of X-Game sports on the demise of legacy sports. Snowboarding, skateboarding, motor cross, and snowmobile racing have also caught the attention of our youth. And how about video gaming? Some colleges are even considering making video gaming a varsity sport. This "Stupid Man" would say, "Are you kidding me?"

I can't argue with the injury issues. Concussions have been pushed forward in our social consciousness, so any contact sports are going to suffer. As far as Lacrosse being on the rise; I am all for that. I probably would have considered playing Lacrosse myself when I was in school if it was available. I actually hope my grandson plays it someday; I will be a huge fan!

I have read articles and listened to Sports Radio shows that discuss the demise of football and how it might go by the wayside in the not-too-distant future. I don't think the NFL has anything to worry about. Even though there are a lot of people who don't want their sons to play football, they still want to watch it and they are willing to spend big money for the privilege. As long as people are willing to pay to watch and stadiums continue to get built, the NFL will thrive. It's similar to way back when nobody really wanted to be a gladiator but a lot of people wanted to see the gladiators compete. NFL players are our modern-day gladiators and, just as early gladiators were criminals, a lot of our NFL players are also.

11/10/2015

So that is it. I have written my third book. This will probably be the end of the line for the "Stupid Man" run, so that officially makes the three books a trilogy. I hope to write other books, but the concepts will change.

Since I am confident there will be no more "Stupid Man" books, I want to close with a couple of reminders. Don't be afraid to remind my family members if you know any of them.

1] I want to be cremated when I die. I am a registered donor, though, so if I have any organs worth saving, get that taken care of first; thanks.

2] Where to scatter my ashes in no particular order: Ely Memorial Baseball Field (Left hand batter's box, pitcher's mound, and over the right field fence), Bemidji State Baseball Field (pitcher's mound), Hibbing CC gym floor, Central Lakes College gym floor, off the deck at the Pink Pony in Gulf Shores, AL, outside of the side door at the Winton Roadhouse, and on Fall Lake out in front of our cabin. The rest can be placed with my wife in her plot at the Ely Cemetery.

3] If there is a funeral, the songs I want played are:
"Knocking on Heaven's Door" by Bob Dylan or Pat Surface
"Moon Shadow" by Cat Stevens
"Just a Gigolo" by David Lee Roth
"The Muppet Show Theme Song" (original version, I'm guessing by the Muppets)
"See You Again" by Carrie Underwood
*I don't want anyone to perform these songs; just play record-

ings.

Don't get the impression I dwell on these things. I don't ask for much. I just want these things to be taken care of, because I won't be around to have any input.

"STILL A STUPID MAN"
MIKE TURNBULL
NOVEMBER 10, 2015

THANK YOUS AND ACKNOWLEDGEMENTS

My Wife, Pam: Thanks for letting me pretend to be an author and send another book to the publisher.

Joany Haag (Co-Owner Winton Roadhouse): Thanks for hosting "Books & Beer" and "Wednesday Nights in Winton." Thanks for the Winton Roadhouse; you guys are doing a great job. I hope the Australia trip goes well. Also, thanks for providing some pictures for this book.

Pat and Donna Surface: Thanks for performing at the Roadhouse in Winton on Wednesday nights all summer. I can't tell you how much Pam and I enjoy it.

Check out Pat and Donna's work on spiritwoodmusic.com and help their fight against Alzheimer's Disease at spiritwoodfoundation.com

Gabby Marano (HCC Volleyball Manager): Thanks for promoting Cardinal Volleyball on the internet and brightening my days. I hope you can also promote this book.

Rod Loe (Father-in-Law): Thanks for making it possible to purchase the cabin.

Lexie and Jeff Baack (Daughter and Son-in-Law): Thanks for getting it right and bringing our first grandchild into our lives. Great job!

Linda Filonowich (Friend): Wrote her first book, *Ginalocks and the Three Fishes*. Great job; outstanding children's book.

Rivershore Books and Jansina: Thanks for having the faith to publish another book for me.

Dr. Rich Mahogany: I recently discovered this website on an advertisement in a public restroom in Michigan. All "Stupid Men" should check this out: mantherapy.org

Family, Players and Students: You are what makes my life as blessed as it is.

PRAYERS

<u>Gerry Levos (A Very Dear Friend):</u> I know very few of you who read this book know Gerry. Just pray that Gerry recovers from her ailment and gets back to being Gerry. She is a very special woman and we all need a "Gerry" in our lives.

<u>Tom Lange and Family:</u> Special guy and great family. Please pray that they deal with their hardship in the best possible manner.

<u>Patricia Turnbull (Mom):</u> Pray she continues to deal with the pain she continues to deal with.

<u>Rod and Tootsie Loe (In-Laws):</u> We still have several years to spend together in Ely. Be healthy and stay in our lives.

<u>Blaine and Alex:</u> Pray for them to have a happy and rich marriage.

<u>Joan Wirtanen (Very Dear Friend):</u> Lost her husband of several years this past year. Pray she finds joy every day in the blessings that come her way.

<u>Steve Kruse (Student):</u> Being deployed overseas. Pray for his safe return.

<u>Anyone you want to add. Especially those experiencing terminal illnesses, loss of loved ones, or military deployment:</u> There is power in prayer!

ABOUT THE AUTHOR

(Photo by Mike Flaten)

I am 56 years old and my wife Pam and I have lived in Hibbing, MN, for the past nineteen years. I coach and teach at Hibbing Community College, and Pam runs the Mitchell-Tappan House Bed and Breakfast in Hibbing. Pam and I own and live in the B&B, but she is the Innkeeper and I claim to be the Groundskeeper. Either way, she is the boss and does a great job. Come stay with us sometime. We currently have our house up for sale and are working on a full retirement and moving to our cabin on Fall Lake outside of Winton, MN.

Pam and I have been married for thirty-four years and have two grown children. Lexie (Baack) lives and works in Nebraska as a high school volleyball coach and pianist. Her husband, Jeff, is a farmer. Our grandson, Beckett, is not gainfully employed, but he is only five months old. Our son, Blaine, lives in the Minneapolis area and works in a juvenile detention center at city hall in Minneapolis. He and his fiancé, Alex, will be married this summer.

I have taught and coached all over Minnesota for the past 35 years. I have cherished every minute of my career. I grew up the son of Jack and Patricia Turnbull and have three sisters, Terri, Lisa, and Stacie. My dad was a career Navy man, so we moved all over the country. He retired from the Navy in 1975 and we moved to

Ely, MN, where I started my junior year of high school.

I received my A.A. degree from Vermilion Community College in Ely in 1979; my Bachelor's degree from Bemidji State University in Bemidji, MN, in 1981; and my Master's Degree from the US Sports Academy in Daphne, AL, in 1990.

I had never attempted to write a book until about four years ago. I had thought about it and been encouraged to do so by friends and family members. Now I have written my third book and possibly a fourth by the time you read this. I am very excited to have the opportunity to share these books with you. I hope you enjoy reading them as much as I do writing them. It is truly a humbling experience to put your thoughts into writing and put them out to the public.

In my 56 years on this earth, enough to qualify as an AARP member and senior discounts at most restaurants, I can't pretend to have figured anything out, but I do think I have a somewhat unique story to tell, and I hope it strikes a chord with those of you who read it. I have had these random thoughts for as long as I can remember and I've managed to write a few of them down for you to consider and ponder.

I feel blessed that Rivershore Books has agreed to publish my third book, and I look forward to future projects with them.

I have always taken pride in being referred to as "Coach," second to my favorite titles of "Husband," "Dad," and now "Grandpa Mike." I never dreamed I would see "Author" in front of my name. I am still hoping this will help me gain entry into the "Stupid Man" club, if and when I get to heaven.

"STILL A STUPID MAN"
"Semi-Retired/Semi-Employed and Loving Life"
Mike Turnbull November 10, 2015

BOOKS BY
MIKE TURNBULL

*All published by Rivershore Books

RANDOM THOUGHTS OF A STUPID MAN

MORE RANDOM THOUGHTS OF A STUPID MAN

STILL A STUPID MAN

A GUIDE TO MIDDLE SCHOOL AND BEYOND

Available in e-books and printed versions.

Available at:

www.rivershorebooks.com
www.amazon.com
www.barnesandnoble.com
www.nookpress.com
www.smashwords.com
Piragasis' Northwoods Store: Ely, MN
Mitchell-Tappan House Bed and Breakfast: Hibbing, MN

RIVERSHORE BOOKS

www.rivershorebooks.com
info@rivershorebooks.com
www.facebook.com/rivershore.books
www.twitter.com/rivershorebooks
blog.rivershorebooks.com
forum.rivershorebooks.com

Made in the USA
Monee, IL
10 September 2021

76801853R10046